How to Think Like a Computer Scientist

Learning with Python

How to Think Like a Computer Scientist

Learning with Python

Allen Downey

Jerey Elkner

Chris Meyers

dreamtech PRESS

Green Tea Press

Wellesley, Massachusetts

Edited by Shannon Turlington and Lisa Cutler.

Green Tea Press
1 Grove St.
P.O. Box 812901
Wellesley, MA 02482

The original form of this book is LATEX source code. Compiling this LATEX source has the effect of generating a device-independent representation of a textbook, which can be converted to other formats and printed.

The LATEX source for this book is available from http://www.thinkpython.com

Publisher's Cataloging-in-Publication (provided by Quality Books, Inc.)

Downey, Allen
How to think like a computer scientist: learning with Python / Allen Downey, Jeffrey Elkner, Chris Meyers.–1st ed.
p. cm.
Includes index.
ISBN 0-9716775-0-6
LCCN 2002100618

1. Python (Computer program language) I. Elkner, Jeffrey. II. Meyers, Chris. III. Title

QA76.73.P98D69 2002 005.13'3
QBI02-200031

ISBN: 978-93-5119-814-7

Reprint Edition: 2023

Copies: 1000

Printed at: Nisha Enterprises.

Foreword

By David Beazley

As an educator, researcher, and book author, I am delighted to see the completion of this book. Python is a fun and extremely easy-to-use programming language that has steadily gained in popularity over the last few years. Developed over ten years ago by Guido van Rossum, Python's simple syntax and overall feel is largely derived from ABC, a teaching language that was developed in the 1980's. However, Python was also created to solve real problems and it borrows a wide variety of features from programming languages such as C++, Java, Modula-3, and Scheme. Because of this, one of Python's most remarkable features is its broad appeal to professional software developers, scientists, researchers, artists, and educators.

Despite Python's appeal to many different communities, you may still wonder "why Python?" or "why teach programming with Python?" Answering these questions is no simple task—especially when popular opinion is on the side of more masochistic alternatives such as C++ and Java. However, I think the most direct answer is that programming in Python is simply a lot of fun and more productive.

When I teach computer science courses, I want to cover important concepts in addition to making the material interesting and engaging to students. Unfortunately, there is a tendency for introductory programming courses to focus far too much attention on mathematical abstraction and for students to become frustrated with annoying problems related to low-level details of syntax, compilation, and the enforcement of seemingly arcane rules. Although such abstraction and formalism is important to professional software engineers and students who plan to continue their study of computer science, taking such an approach in an introductory course mostly succeeds in making computer science boring. When I teach a course, I don't want to have a room of uninspired students. I would much rather see them trying to solve interesting problems by exploring different ideas, taking unconventional approaches, breaking the rules, and learning from their mistakes.

In doing so, I don't want to waste half of the semester trying to sort out obscure syntax problems, unintelligible compiler error messages, or the several hundred ways that a program might generate a general protection fault.

One of the reasons why I like Python is that it provides a really nice balance between the practical and the conceptual. Since Python is interpreted, beginners can pick up the language and start doing neat things almost immediately without getting lost in the problems of compilation and linking. Furthermore, Python comes with a large library of modules that can be used to do all sorts of tasks ranging from web-programming to graphics. Having such a practical focus is a great way to engage students and it allows them to complete significant projects. However, Python can also serve as an excellent foundation for introducing important computer science concepts. Since Python fully supports procedures and classes, students can be gradually introduced to topics such as procedural abstraction, data structures, and object-oriented programming—all of which are applicable to later courses on Java or C++. Python even borrows a number of features from functional programming languages and can be used to introduce concepts that would be covered in more detail in courses on Scheme and Lisp.

In reading Jeffrey's preface, I am struck by his comments that Python allowed him to see a "higher level of success and a lower level of frustration" and that he was able to "move faster with better results." Although these comments refer to his introductory course, I sometimes use Python for these exact same reasons in advanced graduate level computer science courses at the University of Chicago. In these courses, I am constantly faced with the daunting task of covering a lot of difficult course material in a blistering nine week quarter. Although it is certainly possible for me to inflict a lot of pain and suffering by using a language like C++, I have often found this approach to be counterproductive—especially when the course is about a topic unrelated to just "programming." I find that using Python allows me to better focus on the actual topic at hand while allowing students to complete substantial class projects.

Although Python is still a young and evolving language, I believe that it has a bright future in education. This book is an important step in that direction.

David Beazley
University of Chicago
Author of the *Python Essential Reference*

Preface

By Jeff Elkner

This book owes its existence to the collaboration made possible by the Internet and the free software movement. Its three authors—a college professor, a high school teacher, and a professional programmer—have yet to meet face to face, but we have been able to work closely together and have been aided by many wonderful folks who have donated their time and energy to helping make this book better.

We think this book is a testament to the benefits and future possibilities of this kind of collaboration, the framework for which has been put in place by Richard Stallman and the Free Software Foundation.

How and why I came to use Python

In 1999, the College Board's Advanced Placement (AP) Computer Science exam was given in C++ for the first time. As in many high schools throughout the country, the decision to change languages had a direct impact on the computer science curriculum at Yorktown High School in Arlington, Virginia, where I teach. Up to this point, Pascal was the language of instruction in both our first-year and AP courses. In keeping with past practice of giving students two years of exposure to the same language, we made the decision to switch to C++ in the first-year course for the 1997-98 school year so that we would be in step with the College Board's change for the AP course the following year.

Two years later, I was convinced that C++ was a poor choice to use for introducing students to computer science. While it is certainly a very powerful programming language, it is also an extremely difficult language to learn and teach. I found myself constantly fighting with C++'s difficult syntax and multiple ways of doing things, and I was losing many students unnecessarily as a result. Convinced there had to be a better language choice for our first-year class, I went looking for an alternative to C++.

I needed a language that would run on the machines in our Linux lab as well as on the Windows and Macintosh platforms most students have at home. I wanted it to be free and available electronically, so that students could use it at home regardless of their income. I wanted a language that was used by professional programmers, and one that had an active developer community around it. It had to support both procedural and object-oriented programming. And most importantly, it had to be easy to learn and teach. When I investigated the choices with these goals in mind, Python stood out as the best candidate for the job.

I asked one of Yorktown's talented students, Matt Ahrens, to give Python a try. In two months he not only learned the language but wrote an application called pyTicket that enabled our staff to report technology problems via the Web. I knew that Matt could not have finished an application of that scale in so short a time in C++, and this accomplishment, combined with Matt's positive assessment of Python, suggested that Python was the solution I was looking for.

Finding a textbook

Having decided to use Python in both of my introductory computer science classes the following year, the most pressing problem was the lack of an available textbook.

Free content came to the rescue. Earlier in the year, Richard Stallman had introduced me to Allen Downey. Both of us had written to Richard expressing an interest in developing free educational content. Allen had already written a first-year computer science textbook, *How to Think Like a Computer Scientist.* When I read this book, I knew immediately that I wanted to use it in my class. It was the clearest and most helpful computer science text I had seen. It emphasized the processes of thought involved in programming rather than the features of a particular language. Reading it immediately made me a better teacher.

How to Think Like a Computer Scientist was not just an excellent book, but it had been released under a GNU public license, which meant it could be used freely and modified to meet the needs of its user. Once I decided to use Python, it occurred to me that I could translate Allen's original Java version of the book into the new language. While I would not have been able to write a textbook on my own, having Allen's book to work from made it possible for me to do so, at the same time demonstrating that the cooperative development model used so well in software could also work for educational content.

Working on this book for the last two years has been rewarding for both my students and me, and my students played a big part in the process. Since I could make instant changes whenever someone found a spelling error or difficult passage, I encouraged them to look for mistakes in the book by giving them a bonus point each time they made a suggestion that resulted in a change in the text. This had the double benefit of encouraging them to read the text more carefully and of getting the text thoroughly reviewed by its most important critics, students using it to learn computer science.

For the second half of the book on object-oriented programming, I knew that someone with more real programming experience than I had would be needed to do it right. The book sat in an unfinished state for the better part of a year until the free software community once again provided the needed means for its completion.

I received an email from Chris Meyers expressing interest in the book. Chris is a professional programmer who started teaching a programming course last year using Python at Lane Community College in Eugene, Oregon. The prospect of teaching the course had led Chris to the book, and he started helping out with it immediately. By the end of the school year he had created a companion project on our website at `http://www.ibiblio.org/obp` called *Python for Fun* and was working with some of my most advanced students as a master teacher, guiding them beyond where I could take them.

Introducing programming with Python

The process of translating and using *How to Think Like a Computer Scientist* for the past two years has confirmed Python's suitability for teaching beginning students. Python greatly simplifies programming examples and makes important programming ideas easier to teach.

The first example from the text illustrates this point. It is the traditional "hello, world" program, which in the C++ version of the book looks like this:

```
#include <iostream.h>

void main()
{
  cout << "Hello, world." << endl;
}
```

in the Python version it becomes:

```
print "Hello, World!"
```

Even though this is a trivial example, the advantages of Python stand out. Yorktown's Computer Science I course has no prerequisites, so many of the students seeing this example are looking at their first program. Some of them are undoubtedly a little nervous, having heard that computer programming is difficult to learn. The C++ version has always forced me to choose between two unsatisfying options: either to explain `#include`, `void main()`, {, and }, and risk confusing or intimidating some of the students right at the start, or to tell them, "Just don't worry about all of that stuff now; we will talk about it later," and risk the same thing. The educational objectives at this point in the course are to introduce students to the idea of a programming language and to get them to write their first program, thereby introducing them to the programming environment. The Python program has exactly what is needed to do these things, and nothing more.

Comparing the explanatory text of the program in each version of the book further illustrates what this means to the beginning student. There are thirteen paragraphs of explanation of "Hello, world!" in the C++ version; in the Python version, there are only two. More importantly, the missing eleven paragraphs do not deal with the "big ideas" in computer programming but with the minutia of C++ syntax. I found this same thing happening throughout the book. Whole paragraphs simply disappear from the Python version of the text because Python's much clearer syntax renders them unnecessary.

Using a very high-level language like Python allows a teacher to postpone talking about low-level details of the machine until students have the background that they need to better make sense of the details. It thus creates the ability to put "first things first" pedagogically. One of the best examples of this is the way in which Python handles variables. In C++ a variable is a name for a place that holds a thing. Variables have to be declared with types at least in part because the size of the place to which they refer needs to be predetermined. Thus, the idea of a variable is bound up with the hardware of the machine. The powerful and fundamental concept of a variable is already difficult enough for beginning students (in both computer science and algebra). Bytes and addresses do not help the matter. In Python a variable is a name that refers to a thing. This is a far more intuitive concept for beginning students and is much closer to the meaning of "variable" that they learned in their math courses. I had much less difficulty teaching variables this year than I did in the past, and I spent less time helping students with problems using them.

Another example of how Python aids in the teaching and learning of programming is in its syntax for functions. My students have always had a great deal of difficulty understanding functions. The main problem centers around the difference between a function definition and a function call, and the related distinction between a parameter and an argument. Python comes to the rescue with syntax that is nothing short of beautiful. Function definitions begin with the keyword `def`, so I simply tell my students, "When you define a function, begin with `def`, followed by the name of the function that you are defining; when you call a function, simply call (type) out its name." Parameters go with definitions; arguments go with calls. There are no return types, parameter types, or reference and value parameters to get in the way, so I am now able to teach functions in less than half the time that it previously took me, with better comprehension.

Using Python has improved the effectiveness of our computer science program for all students. I see a higher general level of success and a lower level of frustration than I experienced during the two years I taught C++. I move faster with better results. More students leave the course with the ability to create meaningful programs and with the positive attitude toward the experience of programming that this engenders.

Building a community

I have received email from all over the globe from people using this book to learn or to teach programming. A user community has begun to emerge, and many people have been contributing to the project by sending in materials for the companion website at `http://www.thinkpython.com`.

With the publication of the book in print form, I expect the growth in the user community to continue and accelerate. The emergence of this user community and the possibility it suggests for similar collaboration among educators have been the most exciting parts of working on this project for me. By working together, we can increase the quality of materials available for our use and save valuable time. I invite you to join our community and look forward to hearing from you. Please write to the authors at `feedback@thinkpython.com`.

Jeffrey Elkner
Yorktown High School
Arlington, Virginia

Contributor List

To paraphrase the philosophy of the Free Software Foundation, this book is free like free speech, but not necessarily free like free pizza. It came about because of a collaboration that would not have been possible without the GNU Free Documentation License. So we thank the Free Software Foundation for developing this license and, of course, making it available to us.

We also thank the more than 100 sharp-eyed and thoughtful readers who have sent us suggestions and corrections over the past few years. In the spirit of free software, we decided to express our gratitude in the form of a contributor list. Unfortunately, this list is not complete, but we are doing our best to keep it up to date.

If you have a chance to look through the list, you should realize that each person here has spared you and all subsequent readers from the confusion of a technical error or a less-than-transparent explanation, just by sending us a note.

Impossible as it may seem after so many corrections, there may still be errors in this book. If you should stumble across one, please check the online version of the book at `http://thinkpython.com`, which is the most up-to-date version. If the error has not been corrected, please take a minute to send us email at `feedback@thinkpython.com`. If we make a change due to your suggestion, you will appear in the next version of the contributor list (unless you ask to be omitted). Thank you!

- Lloyd Hugh Allen sent in a correction to Section 8.4.
- Yvon Boulianne sent in a correction of a semantic error in Chapter 5.
- Fred Bremmer submitted a correction in Section 2.1.
- Jonah Cohen wrote the Perl scripts to convert the LaTeX source for this book into beautiful HTML.

- Michael Conlon sent in a grammar correction in Chapter 2 and an improvement in style in Chapter 1, and he initiated discussion on the technical aspects of interpreters.
- Benoit Girard sent in a correction to a humorous mistake in Section 5.6.
- Courtney Gleason and Katherine Smith wrote `horsebet.py`, which was used as a case study in an earlier version of the book. Their program can now be found on the website.
- Lee Harr submitted more corrections than we have room to list here, and indeed he should be listed as one of the principal editors of the text.
- James Kaylin is a student using the text. He has submitted numerous corrections.
- David Kershaw fixed the broken `catTwice` function in Section 3.10.
- Eddie Lam has sent in numerous corrections to Chapters 1, 2, and 3. He also fixed the Makefile so that it creates an index the first time it is run and helped us set up a versioning scheme.
- Man-Yong Lee sent in a correction to the example code in Section 2.4.
- David Mayo pointed out that the word "unconsciously" in Chapter 1 needed to be changed to "subconsciously".
- Chris McAloon sent in several corrections to Sections 3.9 and 3.10.
- Matthew J. Moelter has been a long-time contributor who sent in numerous corrections and suggestions to the book.
- Simon Dicon Montford reported a missing function definition and several typos in Chapter 3. He also found errors in the `increment` function in Chapter 13.
- John Ouzts corrected the definition of "return value" in Chapter 3.
- Kevin Parks sent in valuable comments and suggestions as to how to improve the distribution of the book.
- David Pool sent in a typo in the glossary of Chapter 1, as well as kind words of encouragement.
- Michael Schmitt sent in a correction to the chapter on files and exceptions.
- Robin Shaw pointed out an error in Section 13.1, where the printTime function was used in an example without being defined.

- Paul Sleigh found an error in Chapter 7 and a bug in Jonah Cohen's Perl script that generates HTML from LaTeX.
- Craig T. Snydal is testing the text in a course at Drew University. He has contributed several valuable suggestions and corrections.
- Ian Thomas and his students are using the text in a programming course. They are the first ones to test the chapters in the latter half of the book, and they have made numerous corrections and suggestions.
- Keith Verheyden sent in a correction in Chapter 3.
- Peter Winstanley let us know about a longstanding error in our Latin in Chapter 3.
- Chris Wrobel made corrections to the code in the chapter on file I/O and exceptions.
- Moshe Zadka has made invaluable contributions to this project. In addition to writing the first draft of the chapter on Dictionaries, he provided continual guidance in the early stages of the book.
- Christoph Zwerschke sent several corrections and pedagogic suggestions, and explained the difference between *gleich* and *selbe*.
- James Mayer sent us a whole slew of spelling and typographical errors, including two in the contributor list.
- Hayden McAfee caught a potentially confusing inconsistency between two examples.
- Angel Arnal is part of an international team of translators working on the Spanish version of the text. He has also found several errors in the English version.
- Tauhidul Hoque and Lex Berezhny created the illustrations in Chapter 1 and improved many of the other illustrations.
- Dr. Michele Alzetta caught an error in Chapter 8 and sent some interesting pedagogic comments and suggestions about Fibonacci and Old Maid.
- Andy Mitchell caught a typo in Chapter 1 and a broken example in Chapter 2.
- Kalin Harvey suggested a clarification in Chapter 7 and caught some typos.
- Christopher P. Smith caught several typos and is helping us prepare to update the book for Python 2.2.

- David Hutchins caught a typo in the Foreword.
- Gregor Lingl is teaching Python at a high school in Vienna, Austria. He is working on a German translation of the book, and he caught a couple of bad errors in Chapter 5.
- Julie Peters caught a typo in the Preface.
- Florin Oprina sent in an improvement in `makeTime`, a correction in `printTime`, and a nice typo.
- D. J. Webre suggested a clarification in Chapter 3.
- Ken found a fistful of errors in Chapters 8, 9 and 11.
- Ivo Wever caught a typo in Chapter 5 and suggested a clarification in Chapter 3.
- Curtis Yanko suggested a clarification in Chapter 2.
- Ben Logan sent in a number of typos and problems with translating the book into HTML.
- Jason Armstrong saw the missing word in Chapter 2.
- Louis Cordier noticed a spot in Chapter 16 where the code didn't match the text.
- Brian Cain suggested several clarifications in Chapters 2 and 3.
- Rob Black sent in a passel of corrections, including some changes for Python 2.2.
- Jean-Philippe Rey at Ecole Centrale Paris sent a number of patches, including some updates for Python 2.2 and other thoughtful improvements.
- Jason Mader at George Washington University made a number of useful suggestions and corrections.
- Jan Gundtofte-Bruun reminded us that "a error" is an error.
- Abel David and Alexis Dinno reminded us that the plural of "matrix" is "matrices", not "matrixes". This error was in the book for years, but two readers with the same initials reported it on the same day. Weird.
- Charles Thayer encouraged us to get rid of the semi-colons we had put at the ends of some statements and to clean up our use of "argument" and "parameter".

- Roger Sperberg pointed out a twisted piece of logic in Chapter 3.
- Sam Bull pointed out a confusing paragraph in Chapter 2.
- Andrew Cheung pointed out two instances of "use before def."
- Hans Batra found an error in Chapter 16.
- Chris Seberino suggested some improvements in the Preface.
- Yuri Takhteyev pointed out a problem with single and double quotes.

Contents

Foreword v

Preface vii

Contributor List xiii

1 The way of the program 1

1.1 The Python programming language 1

1.2 What is a program? 3

1.3 What is debugging? 4

1.4 Formal and natural languages 6

1.5 The first program 8

1.6 Glossary 8

2 Variables, expressions and statements 11

2.1 Values and types 11

2.2 Variables 12

2.3 Variable names and keywords 13

2.4 Statements 15

2.5 Evaluating expressions 16

2.6 Operators and operands 17

2.7 Order of operations 17

2.8 Operations on strings 18

2.9 Composition 19

2.10 Comments 19

2.11 Glossary 20

3 Functions **23**

3.1 Function calls 23

3.2 Type conversion 24

3.3 Type coercion 24

3.4 Math functions 25

3.5 Composition 26

3.6 Adding new functions 26

3.7 Definitions and use 29

3.8 Flow of execution 29

3.9 Parameters and arguments 30

3.10 Variables and parameters are local 31

3.11 Stack diagrams 32

3.12 Functions with results 33

3.13 Glossary 34

4 Conditionals and recursion **37**

4.1 The modulus operator 37

4.2 Boolean expressions 37

4.3 Logical operators 38

4.4 Conditional execution 39

4.5 Alternative execution 39

4.6 Chained conditionals 40

4.7 Nested conditionals . . . 41
4.8 The `return` statement . . . 42
4.9 Recursion . . . 42
4.10 Stack diagrams for recursive functions . . . 44
4.11 Infinite recursion . . . 45
4.12 Keyboard input . . . 45
4.13 Glossary . . . 46

5 Fruitful functions **49**
5.1 Return values . . . 49
5.2 Program development . . . 50
5.3 Composition . . . 53
5.4 Boolean functions . . . 54
5.5 More recursion . . . 55
5.6 Leap of faith . . . 57
5.7 One more example . . . 58
5.8 Checking types . . . 58
5.9 Glossary . . . 60

6 Iteration **61**
6.1 Multiple assignment . . . 61
6.2 The `while` statement . . . 62
6.3 Tables . . . 64
6.4 Two-dimensional tables . . . 66
6.5 Encapsulation and generalization . . . 67
6.6 More encapsulation . . . 68
6.7 Local variables . . . 69
6.8 More generalization . . . 70
6.9 Functions . . . 71
6.10 Glossary . . . 72

7 Strings 73

7.1 A compound data type . . . 73

7.2 Length . . . 74

7.3 Traversal and the `for` loop . . . 74

7.4 String slices . . . 76

7.5 String comparison . . . 76

7.6 Strings are immutable . . . 77

7.7 A `find` function . . . 78

7.8 Looping and counting . . . 78

7.9 The `string` module . . . 79

7.10 Character classification . . . 80

7.11 Glossary . . . 81

8 Lists 83

8.1 List values . . . 83

8.2 Accessing elements . . . 84

8.3 List length . . . 85

8.4 List membership . . . 86

8.5 Lists and `for` loops . . . 86

8.6 List operations . . . 87

8.7 List slices . . . 88

8.8 Lists are mutable . . . 88

8.9 List deletion . . . 89

8.10 Objects and values . . . 91

8.11 Aliasing . . . 92

8.12 Cloning lists . . . 92

8.13 List parameters . . . 93

8.14 Nested lists . . . 94

8.15 Matrices 94
8.16 Strings and lists 95
8.17 Glossary 96

9 Tuples **97**
9.1 Mutability and tuples 97
9.2 Tuple assignment 98
9.3 Tuples as return values 99
9.4 Random numbers 99
9.5 List of random numbers 100
9.6 Counting 101
9.7 Many buckets 102
9.8 A single-pass solution 104
9.9 Glossary 105

10 Dictionaries **107**
10.1 Dictionary operations 108
10.2 Dictionary methods 109
10.3 Aliasing and copying 110
10.4 Sparse matrices 110
10.5 Hints 111
10.6 Long integers 113
10.7 Counting letters 113
10.8 Glossary 114

11 Files and exceptions **117**
11.1 Text files 119
11.2 Writing variables 120
11.3 Directories 123

11.4 Pickling 123
11.5 Exceptions 124
11.6 Glossary 126

12 Classes and objects **129**
12.1 User-defined compound types 129
12.2 Attributes 130
12.3 Instances as arguments 131
12.4 Sameness 131
12.5 Rectangles 133
12.6 Instances as return values 134
12.7 Objects are mutable 134
12.8 Copying 135
12.9 Glossary 137

13 Classes and functions **139**
13.1 Time 139
13.2 Pure functions 140
13.3 Modifiers 141
13.4 Which is better? 142
13.5 Prototype development versus planning 143
13.6 Generalization 144
13.7 Algorithms 144
13.8 Glossary 145

14 Classes and methods **147**
14.1 Object-oriented features 147
14.2 `printTime` 148
14.3 Another example 149

14.4 A more complicated example 150

14.5 Optional arguments 151

14.6 The initialization method 152

14.7 Points revisited 153

14.8 Operator overloading 154

14.9 Polymorphism 155

14.10 Glossary 157

15 Sets of objects **159**

15.1 Composition 159

15.2 `Card` objects 159

15.3 Class attributes and the `__str__` method 161

15.4 Comparing cards 162

15.5 Decks 163

15.6 Printing the deck 163

15.7 Shuffling the deck 165

15.8 Removing and dealing cards 166

15.9 Glossary 167

16 Inheritance **169**

16.1 Inheritance 169

16.2 A hand of cards 170

16.3 Dealing cards 171

16.4 Printing a Hand 171

16.5 The `CardGame` class 172

16.6 `OldMaidHand` class 173

16.7 `OldMaidGame` class 175

16.8 Glossary 179

17 Linked lists **181**

17.1 Embedded references 181

17.2 The `Node` class 181

17.3 Lists as collections 183

17.4 Lists and recursion 184

17.5 Infinite lists 185

17.6 The fundamental ambiguity theorem 186

17.7 Modifying lists 186

17.8 Wrappers and helpers 187

17.9 The `LinkedList` class 188

17.10 Invariants 189

17.11 Glossary 190

18 Stacks **191**

18.1 Abstract data types 191

18.2 The Stack ADT 192

18.3 Implementing stacks with Python lists 192

18.4 Pushing and popping 193

18.5 Using a stack to evaluate postfix 194

18.6 Parsing 194

18.7 Evaluating postfix 195

18.8 Clients and providers 196

18.9 Glossary 197

19 Queues **199**

19.1 The Queue ADT 199

19.2 Linked Queue 200

19.3 Performance characteristics 201

19.4 Improved Linked Queue 201
19.5 Priority queue 203
19.6 The `Golfer` class 205
19.7 Glossary 206

20 Trees **207**
20.1 Building trees 208
20.2 Traversing trees 209
20.3 Expression trees 209
20.4 Tree traversal 210
20.5 Building an expression tree 212
20.6 Handling errors 216
20.7 The animal tree 216
20.8 Glossary 219

A Debugging **221**
A.1 Syntax errors 221
A.2 Runtime errors 223
A.3 Semantic errors 227

B Creating a new data type **231**
B.1 Fraction multiplication 232
B.2 Fraction addition 234
B.3 Euclid's algorithm 234
B.4 Comparing fractions 235
B.5 Taking it further 236
B.6 Glossary 236

C Recommendations for further reading **239**
C.1 Python-related web sites and books 240
C.2 Recommended general computer science books 241

Chapter 1

The way of the program

The goal of this book is to teach you to think like a computer scientist. This way of thinking combines some of the best features of mathematics, engineering, and natural science. Like mathematicians, computer scientists use formal languages to denote ideas (specifically computations). Like engineers, they design things, assembling components into systems and evaluating tradeoffs among alternatives. Like scientists, they observe the behavior of complex systems, form hypotheses, and test predictions.

The single most important skill for a computer scientist is **problem solving**. Problem solving means the ability to formulate problems, think creatively about solutions, and express a solution clearly and accurately. As it turns out, the process of learning to program is an excellent opportunity to practice problem-solving skills. That's why this chapter is called, "The way of the program."

On one level, you will be learning to program, a useful skill by itself. On another level, you will use programming as a means to an end. As we go along, that end will become clearer.

1.1 The Python programming language

The programming language you will be learning is Python. Python is an example of a **high-level language**; other high-level languages you might have heard of are C, C++, Perl, and Java.

As you might infer from the name "high-level language," there are also **low-level languages**, sometimes referred to as "machine languages" or "assembly languages." Loosely speaking, computers can only execute programs written in low-level languages. Thus, programs written in a high-level language have to be processed before they can run. This extra processing takes some time, which is a small disadvantage of high-level languages.

But the advantages are enormous. First, it is much easier to program in a high-level language. Programs written in a high-level language take less time to write, they are shorter and easier to read, and they are more likely to be correct. Second, high-level languages are **portable**, meaning that they can run on different kinds of computers with few or no modifications. Low-level programs can run on only one kind of computer and have to be rewritten to run on another.

Due to these advantages, almost all programs are written in high-level languages. Low-level languages are used only for a few specialized applications.

Two kinds of programs process high-level languages into low-level languages: **interpreters** and **compilers**. An interpreter reads a high-level program and executes it, meaning that it does what the program says. It processes the program a little at a time, alternately reading lines and performing computations.

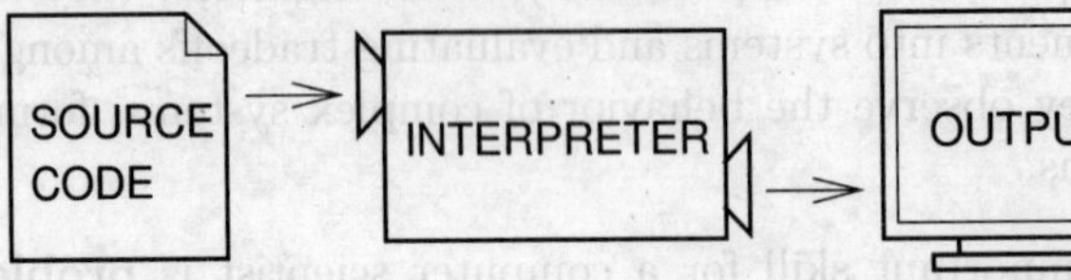

A compiler reads the program and translates it completely before the program starts running. In this case, the high-level program is called the **source code**, and the translated program is called the **object code** or the **executable**. Once a program is compiled, you can execute it repeatedly without further translation.

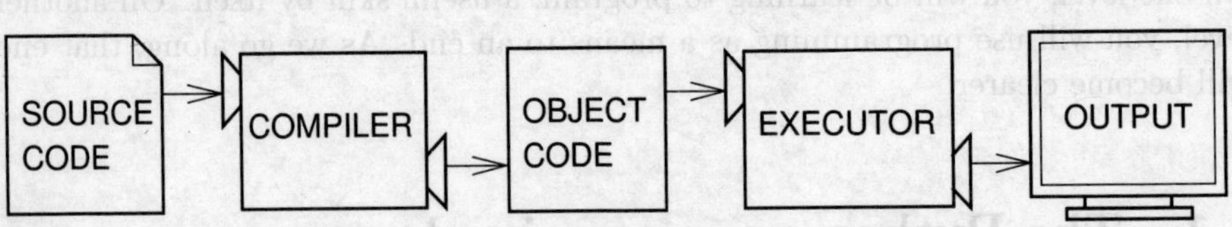

Python is considered an interpreted language because Python programs are executed by an interpreter. There are two ways to use the interpreter: command-line mode and script mode. In command-line mode, you type Python programs and the interpreter prints the result:

```
$ python
Python 2.4.1 (#1, Apr 29 2005, 00:28:56)
Type "help", "copyright", "credits" or "license" for more information.
>>> print 1 + 1
2
```

The first line of this example is the command that starts the Python interpreter. The next two lines are messages from the interpreter. The third line starts with `>>>`, which is the prompt the interpreter uses to indicate that it is ready. We typed `print 1 + 1`, and the interpreter replied 2.

Alternatively, you can write a program in a file and use the interpreter to execute the contents of the file. Such a file is called a **script**. For example, we used a text editor to create a file named `latoya.py` with the following contents:

```
print 1 + 1
```

By convention, files that contain Python programs have names that end with `.py`.

To execute the program, we have to tell the interpreter the name of the script:

```
$ python latoya.py
2
```

In other development environments, the details of executing programs may differ. Also, most programs are more interesting than this one.

Most of the examples in this book are executed on the command line. Working on the command line is convenient for program development and testing, because you can type programs and execute them immediately. Once you have a working program, you should store it in a script so you can execute or modify it in the future.

1.2 What is a program?

A **program** is a sequence of instructions that specifies how to perform a computation. The computation might be something mathematical, such as solving a system of equations or finding the roots of a polynomial, but it can also be a symbolic computation, such as searching and replacing text in a document or (strangely enough) compiling a program.

The details look different in different languages, but a few basic instructions appear in just about every language:

input: Get data from the keyboard, a file, or some other device.

output: Display data on the screen or send data to a file or other device.

math: Perform basic mathematical operations like addition and multiplication.

conditional execution: Check for certain conditions and execute the appropriate sequence of statements.

repetition: Perform some action repeatedly, usually with some variation.

Believe it or not, that's pretty much all there is to it. Every program you've ever used, no matter how complicated, is made up of instructions that look more or less like these. Thus, we can describe programming as the process of breaking a large, complex task into smaller and smaller subtasks until the subtasks are simple enough to be performed with one of these basic instructions.

That may be a little vague, but we will come back to this topic later when we talk about **algorithms**.

1.3 What is debugging?

Programming is a complex process, and because it is done by human beings, it often leads to errors. For whimsical reasons, programming errors are called **bugs** and the process of tracking them down and correcting them is called **debugging**.

Three kinds of errors can occur in a program: syntax errors, runtime errors, and semantic errors. It is useful to distinguish between them in order to track them down more quickly.

1.3.1 Syntax errors

Python can only execute a program if the program is syntactically correct; otherwise, the process fails and returns an error message. **Syntax** refers to the structure of a program and the rules about that structure. For example, in English, a sentence must begin with a capital letter and end with a period. this sentence contains a **syntax error**. So does this one

For most readers, a few syntax errors are not a significant problem, which is why we can read the poetry of e. e. cummings without spewing error messages. Python is not so forgiving. If there is a single syntax error anywhere in your program, Python will print an error message and quit, and you will not be able to run your program. During the first few weeks of your programming career, you will probably spend a lot of time tracking down syntax errors. As you gain experience, though, you will make fewer errors and find them faster.

1.3.2 Runtime errors

The second type of error is a runtime error, so called because the error does not appear until you run the program. These errors are also called **exceptions** because they usually indicate that something exceptional (and bad) has happened.

Runtime errors are rare in the simple programs you will see in the first few chapters, so it might be a while before you encounter one.

1.3.3 Semantic errors

The third type of error is the **semantic error**. If there is a semantic error in your program, it will run successfully, in the sense that the computer will not generate any error messages, but it will not do the right thing. It will do something else. Specifically, it will do what you told it to do.

The problem is that the program you wrote is not the program you wanted to write. The meaning of the program (its semantics) is wrong. Identifying semantic errors can be tricky because it requires you to work backward by looking at the output of the program and trying to figure out what it is doing.

1.3.4 Experimental debugging

One of the most important skills you will acquire is debugging. Although it can be frustrating, debugging is one of the most intellectually rich, challenging, and interesting parts of programming.

In some ways, debugging is like detective work. You are confronted with clues, and you have to infer the processes and events that led to the results you see.

Debugging is also like an experimental science. Once you have an idea what is going wrong, you modify your program and try again. If your hypothesis was correct, then you can predict the result of the modification, and you take a step closer to a working program. If your hypothesis was wrong, you have to come up with a new one. As Sherlock Holmes pointed out, "When you have eliminated the impossible, whatever remains, however improbable, must be the truth." (A. Conan Doyle, *The Sign of Four*)

For some people, programming and debugging are the same thing. That is, programming is the process of gradually debugging a program until it does what you want. The idea is that you should start with a program that does *something* and make small modifications, debugging them as you go, so that you always have a working program.

For example, Linux is an operating system that contains thousands of lines of code, but it started out as a simple program Linus Torvalds used to explore the Intel 80386 chip. According to Larry Greenfield, "One of Linus's earlier projects was a program that would switch between printing AAAA and BBBB. This later evolved to Linux." (*The Linux Users' Guide* Beta Version 1)

Later chapters will make more suggestions about debugging and other programming practices.

1.4 Formal and natural languages

Natural languages are the languages that people speak, such as English, Spanish, and French. They were not designed by people (although people try to impose some order on them); they evolved naturally.

Formal languages are languages that are designed by people for specific applications. For example, the notation that mathematicians use is a formal language that is particularly good at denoting relationships among numbers and symbols. Chemists use a formal language to represent the chemical structure of molecules. And most importantly:

> **Programming languages are formal languages that have been designed to express computations.**

Formal languages tend to have strict rules about syntax. For example, $3 + 3 = 6$ is a syntactically correct mathematical statement, but 3=+6$ is not. H_2O is a syntactically correct chemical name, but $_2Zz$ is not.

Syntax rules come in two flavors, pertaining to **tokens** and structure. Tokens are the basic elements of the language, such as words, numbers, and chemical elements. One of the problems with 3=+6$ is that $ is not a legal token in mathematics (at least as far as we know). Similarly, $_2Zz$ is not legal because there is no element with the abbreviation Zz.

The second type of syntax error pertains to the structure of a statement—that is, the way the tokens are arranged. The statement 3=+6$ is structurally illegal because you can't place a plus sign immediately after an equal sign. Similarly, molecular formulas have to have subscripts after the element name, not before.

> *As an exercise, create what appears to be a well-structured English sentence with unrecognizable tokens in it. Then write another sentence with all valid tokens but with invalid structure.*

When you read a sentence in English or a statement in a formal language, you have to figure out what the structure of the sentence is (although in a natural language you do this subconsciously). This process is called **parsing**.

For example, when you hear the sentence, "The other shoe fell," you understand that "the other shoe" is the subject and "fell" is the predicate. Once you have parsed a sentence, you can figure out what it means, or the semantics of the sentence. Assuming that you know what a shoe is and what it means to fall, you will understand the general implication of this sentence.

Although formal and natural languages have many features in common—tokens, structure, syntax, and semantics—there are many differences:

ambiguity: Natural languages are full of ambiguity, which people deal with by using contextual clues and other information. Formal languages are designed to be nearly or completely unambiguous, which means that any statement has exactly one meaning, regardless of context.

redundancy: In order to make up for ambiguity and reduce misunderstandings, natural languages employ lots of redundancy. As a result, they are often verbose. Formal languages are less redundant and more concise.

literalness: Natural languages are full of idiom and metaphor. If I say, "The other shoe fell," there is probably no shoe and nothing falling. Formal languages mean exactly what they say.

People who grow up speaking a natural language—everyone—often have a hard time adjusting to formal languages. In some ways, the difference between formal and natural language is like the difference between poetry and prose, but more so:

Poetry: Words are used for their sounds as well as for their meaning, and the whole poem together creates an effect or emotional response. Ambiguity is not only common but often deliberate.

Prose: The literal meaning of words is more important, and the structure contributes more meaning. Prose is more amenable to analysis than poetry but still often ambiguous.

Programs: The meaning of a computer program is unambiguous and literal, and can be understood entirely by analysis of the tokens and structure.

Here are some suggestions for reading programs (and other formal languages). First, remember that formal languages are much more dense than natural languages, so it takes longer to read them. Also, the structure is very important, so it is usually not a good idea to read from top to bottom, left to right. Instead, learn to parse the program in your head, identifying the tokens and interpreting the structure. Finally, the details matter. Little things like spelling errors and bad punctuation, which you can get away with in natural languages, can make a big difference in a formal language.

1.5 The first program

Traditionally, the first program written in a new language is called "Hello, World!" because all it does is display the words, "Hello, World!" In Python, it looks like this:

```
print "Hello, World!"
```

This is an example of a **print statement**, which doesn't actually print anything on paper. It displays a value on the screen. In this case, the result is the words

```
Hello, World!
```

The quotation marks in the program mark the beginning and end of the value; they don't appear in the result.

Some people judge the quality of a programming language by the simplicity of the "Hello, World!" program. By this standard, Python does about as well as possible.

1.6 Glossary

problem solving: The process of formulating a problem, finding a solution, and expressing the solution.

high-level language: A programming language like Python that is designed to be easy for humans to read and write.

low-level language: A programming language that is designed to be easy for a computer to execute; also called "machine language" or "assembly language."

portability: A property of a program that can run on more than one kind of computer.

interpret: To execute a program in a high-level language by translating it one line at a time.

compile: To translate a program written in a high-level language into a low-level language all at once, in preparation for later execution.

source code: A program in a high-level language before being compiled.

object code: The output of the compiler after it translates the program.

executable: Another name for object code that is ready to be executed.

script: A program stored in a file (usually one that will be interpreted).

program: A set of instructions that specifies a computation.

algorithm: A general process for solving a category of problems.

bug: An error in a program.

debugging: The process of finding and removing any of the three kinds of programming errors.

syntax: The structure of a program.

syntax error: An error in a program that makes it impossible to parse (and therefore impossible to interpret).

runtime error: An error that does not occur until the program has started to execute but that prevents the program from continuing.

exception: Another name for a runtime error.

semantic error: An error in a program that makes it do something other than what the programmer intended.

semantics: The meaning of a program.

natural language: Any one of the languages that people speak that evolved naturally.

formal language: Any one of the languages that people have designed for specific purposes, such as representing mathematical ideas or computer programs; all programming languages are formal languages.

token: One of the basic elements of the syntactic structure of a program, analogous to a word in a natural language.

parse: To examine a program and analyze the syntactic structure.

print statement: An instruction that causes the Python interpreter to display a value on the screen.

source code: A program in a high-level language before being compiled.

object code: The output of the compiler after it translates the program.

executable: Another name for object code that is ready to be executed.

script: A program stored in a file (usually one that will be interpreted).

program: A set of instructions that specifies a computation.

algorithm: A general process for solving a category of problems.

bug: An error in a program.

debugging: The process of finding and removing any of the three kinds of programming errors.

syntax: The structure of a program.

syntax error: An error in a program that makes it impossible to parse (and therefore impossible to interpret).

runtime error: An error that does not occur until the program has started to execute but that prevents the program from continuing.

exception: Another name for a runtime error.

semantic error: An error in a program that makes it do something other than what the programmer intended.

semantics: The meaning of a program.

natural language: Any one of the languages that people speak that evolved naturally.

formal language: Any one of the languages that people have designed for specific purposes, such as representing mathematical ideas or computer programs; all programming languages are formal languages.

token: One of the basic elements of the syntactic structure of a program, analogous to a word in a natural language.

parse: To examine a program and analyze the syntactic structure.

print statement: An instruction that causes the Python interpreter to display a value on the screen.

Chapter 2

Variables, expressions and statements

2.1 Values and types

A **value** is one of the fundamental things—like a letter or a number—that a program manipulates. The values we have seen so far are `2` (the result when we added `1 + 1`), and `'Hello, World!'`.

These values belong to different **types**: `2` is an integer, and `'Hello, World!'` is a **string**, so-called because it contains a "string" of letters. You (and the interpreter) can identify strings because they are enclosed in quotation marks.

The print statement also works for integers.

```
>>> print 4
4
```

If you are not sure what type a value has, the interpreter can tell you.

```
>>> type('Hello, World!')
<type 'str'>
>>> type(17)
<type 'int'>
```

Not surprisingly, strings belong to the type `str` and integers belong to the type `int`. Less obviously, numbers with a decimal point belong to a type called `float`, because these numbers are represented in a format called **floating-point**.

```
>>> type(3.2)
<type 'float'>
```

What about values like `'17'` and `'3.2'`? They look like numbers, but they are in quotation marks like strings.

```
>>> type('17')
<type 'str'>
>>> type('3.2')
<type 'str'>
```

They're strings.

When you type a large integer, you might be tempted to use commas between groups of three digits, as in `1,000,000`. This is not a legal integer in Python, but it is a legal expression:

```
>>> print 1,000,000
1 0 0
```

Well, that's not what we expected at all! Python interprets `1,000,000` as a comma-separated list of three integers, which it prints consecutively. This is the first example we have seen of a semantic error: the code runs without producing an error message, but it doesn't do the "right" thing.

2.2 Variables

One of the most powerful features of a programming language is the ability to manipulate **variables**. A variable is a name that refers to a value.

The **assignment statement** creates new variables and gives them values:

```
>>> message = "What's up, Doc?"
>>> n = 17
>>> pi = 3.14159
```

This example makes three assignments. The first assigns the string `"What's up, Doc?"` to a new variable named `message`. The second gives the integer `17` to `n`, and the third gives the floating-point number `3.14159` to `pi`.

Notice that the first statement uses double quotes to enclose the string. In general, single and double quotes do the same thing, but if the string contains a single quote (or an apostrophe, which is the same character), you have to use double quotes to enclose it.

A common way to represent variables on paper is to write the name with an arrow pointing to the variable's value. This kind of figure is called a **state diagram** because it shows what state each of the variables is in (think of it as the variable's state of mind). This diagram shows the result of the assignment statements:

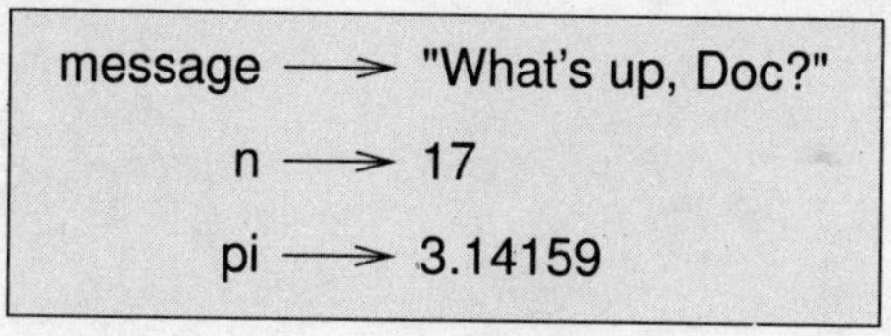

The print statement also works with variables.

```
>>> print message
What's up, Doc?
>>> print n
17
>>> print pi
3.14159
```

In each case the result is the value of the variable. Variables also have types; again, we can ask the interpreter what they are.

```
>>> type(message)
<type 'str'>
>>> type(n)
<type 'int'>
>>> type(pi)
<type 'float'>
```

The type of a variable is the type of the value it refers to.

2.3 Variable names and keywords

Programmers generally choose names for their variables that are meaningful—they document what the variable is used for.

Variable names can be arbitrarily long. They can contain both letters and numbers, but they have to begin with a letter. Although it is legal to use uppercase letters, by convention we don't. If you do, remember that case matters. `Bruce` and `bruce` are different variables.

The underscore character (_) can appear in a name. It is often used in names with multiple words, such as `my_name` or `price_of_tea_in_china`.

If you give a variable an illegal name, you get a syntax error:

```
>>> 76trombones = 'big parade'
SyntaxError: invalid syntax
>>> more$ = 1000000
SyntaxError: invalid syntax
>>> class = 'Computer Science 101'
SyntaxError: invalid syntax
```

`76trombones` is illegal because it does not begin with a letter. `more$` is illegal because it contains an illegal character, the dollar sign. But what's wrong with `class`?

It turns out that `class` is one of the Python **keywords**. Keywords define the language's rules and structure, and they cannot be used as variable names.

Python has twenty-nine keywords:

```
and       def      exec     if       not      return
assert    del      finally  import   or       try
break     elif     for      in       pass     while
class     else     from     is       print    yield
continue  except   global   lambda   raise
```

You might want to keep this list handy. If the interpreter complains about one of your variable names and you don't know why, see if it is on this list.

2.4 Statements

A statement is an instruction that the Python interpreter can execute. We have seen two kinds of statements: print and assignment.

When you type a statement on the command line, Python executes it and displays the result, if there is one. The result of a print statement is a value. Assignment statements don't produce a result.

A script usually contains a sequence of statements. If there is more than one statement, the results appear one at a time as the statements execute.

For example, the script

```
print 1
x = 2
print x
```

produces the output

```
1
2
```

Again, the assignment statement produces no output.

2.5 Evaluating expressions

An expression is a combination of values, variables, and operators. If you type an expression on the command line, the interpreter **evaluates** it and displays the result:

```
>>> 1 + 1
2
```

Although expressions contain values, variables, and operators, not every expression contains all of these elements. A value all by itself is considered an expression, and so is a variable.

```
>>> 17
17
>>> x
2
```

Confusingly, evaluating an expression is not quite the same thing as printing a value.

```
>>> message = 'Hello, World!'
>>> message
'Hello, World!'
>>> print message
Hello, World!
```

When the Python interpreter displays the value of an expression, it uses the same format you would use to enter a value. In the case of strings, that means that it includes the quotation marks. But if you use a print statement, Python displays the contents of the string without the quotation marks.

In a script, an expression all by itself is a legal statement, but it doesn't do anything. The script

```
17
3.2
'Hello, World!'
1 + 1
```

produces no output at all. How would you change the script to display the values of these four expressions?

2.6 Operators and operands

Operators are special symbols that represent computations like addition and multiplication. The values the operator uses are called **operands**.

The following are all legal Python expressions whose meaning is more or less clear:

```
20+32   hour-1   hour*60+minute   minute/60   5**2   (5+9)*(15-7)
```

The symbols +, -, and /, and the use of parenthesis for grouping, mean in Python what they mean in mathematics. The asterisk (*) is the symbol for multiplication, and ** is the symbol for exponentiation.

When a variable name appears in the place of an operand, it is replaced with its value before the operation is performed.

Addition, subtraction, multiplication, and exponentiation all do what you expect, but you might be surprised by division. The following operation has an unexpected result:

```
>>> minute = 59
>>> minute/60
0
```

The value of `minute` is 59, and in conventional arithmetic 59 divided by 60 is 0.98333, not 0. The reason for the discrepancy is that Python is performing **integer division**.

When both of the operands are integers, the result must also be an integer, and by convention, integer division always rounds *down*, even in cases like this where the next integer is very close.

A possible solution to this problem is to calculate a percentage rather than a fraction:

```
>>> minute*100/60
98
```

Again the result is rounded down, but at least now the answer is approximately correct. Another alternative is to use floating-point division, which we get to in Chapter 3.

2.7 Order of operations

When more than one operator appears in an expression, the order of evaluation depends on the **rules of precedence**. Python follows the same precedence rules for its mathematical operators that mathematics does. The acronym **PEMDAS** is a useful way to remember the order of operations:

- Parentheses have the highest precedence and can be used to force an expression to evaluate in the order you want. Since expressions in parentheses are evaluated first, `2 * (3-1)` is 4, and `(1+1)**(5-2)` is 8. You can also use parentheses to make an expression easier to read, as in `(minute * 100) / 60`, even though it doesn't change the result.

- Exponentiation has the next highest precedence, so `2**1+1` is 3 and not 4, and `3*1**3` is 3 and not 27.

- **M**ultiplication and **D**ivision have the same precedence, which is higher than **A**ddition and **S**ubtraction, which also have the same precedence. So `2*3-1` yields 5 rather than 4, and `2/3-1` is `-1`, not `1` (remember that in integer division, `2/3=0`).

- Operators with the same precedence are evaluated from left to right. So in the expression `minute*100/60`, the multiplication happens first, yielding `5900/60`, which in turn yields `98`. If the operations had been evaluated from right to left, the result would have been `59*1`, which is `59`, which is wrong.

2.8 Operations on strings

In general, you cannot perform mathematical operations on strings, even if the strings look like numbers. The following are illegal (assuming that `message` has type `string`):

```
message-1   'Hello'/123   message*'Hello'   '15'+2
```

Interestingly, the `+` operator does work with strings, although it does not do exactly what you might expect. For strings, the `+` operator represents **concatenation**, which means joining the two operands by linking them end-to-end. For example:

```
fruit = 'banana'
bakedGood = ' nut bread'
print fruit + bakedGood
```

The output of this program is `banana nut bread`. The space before the word `nut` is part of the string, and is necessary to produce the space between the concatenated strings.

The `*` operator also works on strings; it performs repetition. For example, `'Fun'*3` is `'FunFunFun'`. One of the operands has to be a string; the other has to be an integer.

On one hand, this interpretation of + and * makes sense by analogy with addition and multiplication. Just as 4*3 is equivalent to 4+4+4, we expect 'Fun'*3 to be the same as 'Fun'+'Fun'+'Fun', and it is. On the other hand, there is a significant way in which string concatenation and repetition are different from integer addition and multiplication. Can you think of a property that addition and multiplication have that string concatenation and repetition do not?

2.9 Composition

So far, we have looked at the elements of a program—variables, expressions, and statements—in isolation, without talking about how to combine them.

One of the most useful features of programming languages is their ability to take small building blocks and **compose** them. For example, we know how to add numbers and we know how to print; it turns out we can do both at the same time:

```
>>>  print 17 + 3
20
```

In reality, the addition has to happen before the printing, so the actions aren't actually happening at the same time. The point is that any expression involving numbers, strings, and variables can be used inside a print statement. You've already seen an example of this:

```
print 'Number of minutes since midnight: ', hour*60+minute
```

You can also put arbitrary expressions on the right-hand side of an assignment statement:

```
percentage = (minute * 100) / 60
```

This ability may not seem impressive now, but you will see other examples where composition makes it possible to express complex computations neatly and concisely.

Warning: There are limits on where you can use certain expressions. For example, the left-hand side of an assignment statement has to be a *variable* name, not an expression. So, the following is illegal: `minute+1 = hour`.

2.10 Comments

As programs get bigger and more complicated, they get more difficult to read. Formal languages are dense, and it is often difficult to look at a piece of code and figure out what it is doing, or why.

For this reason, it is a good idea to add notes to your programs to explain in natural language what the program is doing. These notes are called **comments**, and they are marked with the # symbol:

```
# compute the percentage of the hour that has elapsed
percentage = (minute * 100) / 60
```

In this case, the comment appears on a line by itself. You can also put comments at the end of a line:

```
percentage = (minute * 100) / 60     # caution: integer division
```

Everything from the # to the end of the line is ignored—it has no effect on the program. The message is intended for the programmer or for future programmers who might use this code. In this case, it reminds the reader about the ever-surprising behavior of integer division.

This sort of comment is less necessary if you use the integer division operation, //. It has the same effect as the division operator[1], but it signals that the effect is deliberate.

```
percentage = (minute * 100) // 60
```

The integer division operator is like a comment that says, "I know this is integer division, and I like it that way!"

2.11 Glossary

value: A number or string (or other thing to be named later) that can be stored in a variable or computed in an expression.

type: A set of values. The type of a value determines how it can be used in expressions. So far, the types you have seen are integers (type `int`), floating-point numbers (type `float`), and strings (type `string`).

floating-point: A format for representing numbers with fractional parts.

variable: A name that refers to a value.

statement: A section of code that represents a command or action. So far, the statements you have seen are assignments and print statements.

assignment: A statement that assigns a value to a variable.

[1] For now. The behavior of the division operator may change in future versions of Python.

state diagram: A graphical representation of a set of variables and the values to which they refer.

keyword: A reserved word that is used by the compiler to parse a program; you cannot use keywords like `if`, `def`, and `while` as variable names.

operator: A special symbol that represents a simple computation like addition, multiplication, or string concatenation.

operand: One of the values on which an operator operates.

expression: A combination of variables, operators, and values that represents a single result value.

evaluate: To simplify an expression by performing the operations in order to yield a single value.

integer division: An operation that divides one integer by another and yields an integer. Integer division yields only the whole number of times that the numerator is divisible by the denominator and discards any remainder.

rules of precedence: The set of rules governing the order in which expressions involving multiple operators and operands are evaluated.

concatenate: To join two operands end-to-end.

composition: The ability to combine simple expressions and statements into compound statements and expressions in order to represent complex computations concisely.

comment: Information in a program that is meant for other programmers (or anyone reading the source code) and has no effect on the execution of the program.

state diagram: A graphical representation of a set of variables and the values to which they refer.

keyword: A reserved word that is used by the compiler to parse a program; you cannot use keywords like if, def, and while as variable names.

operator: A special symbol that represents a simple computation like addition, multiplication, or string concatenation.

operand: One of the values on which an operator operates.

expression: A combination of variables, operators, and values that represents a single result value.

evaluate: To simplify an expression by performing the operations in order to yield a single value.

integer division: An operation that divides one integer by another and yields an integer. Integer division yields only the whole number of times that the numerator is divisible by the denominator and discards any remainder.

rules of precedence: The set of rules governing the order in which expressions involving multiple operators and operands are evaluated.

concatenate: To join two operands end-to-end.

composition: The ability to combine simple expressions and statements into compound statements and expressions in order to represent complex computations concisely.

comment: Information in a program that is meant for other programmers (or anyone reading the source code) and has no effect on the execution of the program.

Chapter 3

Functions

3.1 Function calls

You have already seen one example of a **function call**:

```
>>> type("32")
<type 'str'>
```

The name of the function is `type`, and it displays the type of a value or variable. The value or variable, which is called the **argument** of the function, has to be enclosed in parentheses. It is common to say that a function "takes" an argument and "returns" a result. The result is called the **return value**.

Instead of printing the return value, we could assign it to a variable:

```
>>> betty = type("32")
>>> print betty
<type 'str'>
```

As another example, the `id` function takes a value or a variable and returns an integer that acts as a unique identifier for the value:

```
>>> id(3)
134882108
>>> betty = 3
>>> id(betty)
134882108
```

Every value has an `id`, which is a unique number related to where it is stored in the memory of the computer. The `id` of a variable is the `id` of the value to which it refers.

3.2 Type conversion

Python provides a collection of built-in functions that convert values from one type to another. The `int` function takes any value and converts it to an integer, if possible, or complains otherwise:

```
>>> int("32")
32
>>> int("Hello")
ValueError: invalid literal for int(): Hello
```

`int` can also convert floating-point values to integers, but remember that it truncates the fractional part:

```
>>> int(3.99999)
3
>>> int(-2.3)
-2
```

The `float` function converts integers and strings to floating-point numbers:

```
>>> float(32)
32.0
>>> float("3.14159")
3.14159
```

Finally, the `str` function converts to type `string`:

```
>>> str(32)
'32'
>>> str(3.14149)
'3.14149'
```

It may seem odd that Python distinguishes the integer value `1` from the floating-point value `1.0`. They may represent the same number, but they belong to different types. The reason is that they are represented differently inside the computer.

3.3 Type coercion

Now that we can convert between types, we have another way to deal with integer division. Returning to the example from the previous chapter, suppose we want to calculate the fraction of an hour that has elapsed. The most obvious expression, `minute / 60`, does integer arithmetic, so the result is always 0, even at 59 minutes past the hour.

One solution is to convert `minute` to floating-point and do floating-point division:

```
>>> minute = 59
>>> float(minute) / 60
0.983333333333
```

Alternatively, we can take advantage of the rules for automatic type conversion, which is called **type coercion**. For the mathematical operators, if either operand is a `float`, the other is automatically converted to a `float`:

```
>>> minute = 59
>>> minute / 60.0
0.983333333333
```

By making the denominator a `float`, we force Python to do floating-point division.

3.4 Math functions

In mathematics, you have probably seen functions like `sin` and `log`, and you have learned to evaluate expressions like `sin(pi/2)` and `log(1/x)`. First, you evaluate the expression in parentheses (the argument). For example, `pi/2` is approximately 1.571, and `1/x` is 0.1 (if `x` happens to be 10.0).

Then, you evaluate the function itself, either by looking it up in a table or by performing various computations. The `sin` of 1.571 is 1, and the `log` of 0.1 is -1 (assuming that `log` indicates the logarithm base 10).

This process can be applied repeatedly to evaluate more complicated expressions like `log(1/sin(pi/2))`. First, you evaluate the argument of the innermost function, then evaluate the function, and so on.

Python has a math module that provides most of the familiar mathematical functions. A **module** is a file that contains a collection of related functions grouped together.

Before we can use the functions from a module, we have to import them:

```
>>> import math
```

To call one of the functions, we have to specify the name of the module and the name of the function, separated by a dot, also known as a period. This format is called **dot notation**.

```
>>> decibel = math.log10 (17.0)
>>> angle = 1.5
>>> height = math.sin(angle)
```

The first statement sets decibel to the logarithm of 17, base 10. There is also a function called log that takes logarithm base e.

The third statement finds the sine of the value of the variable angle. sin and the other trigonometric functions (cos, tan, etc.) take arguments in radians. To convert from degrees to radians, divide by 360 and multiply by 2*pi. For example, to find the sine of 45 degrees, first calculate the angle in radians and then take the sine:

```
>>> degrees = 45
>>> angle = degrees * 2 * math.pi / 360.0
>>> math.sin(angle)
0.707106781187
```

The constant pi is also part of the math module. If you know your geometry, you can check the previous result by comparing it to the square root of two divided by two:

```
>>> math.sqrt(2) / 2.0
0.707106781187
```

3.5 Composition

Just as with mathematical functions, Python functions can be composed, meaning that you use one expression as part of another. For example, you can use any expression as an argument to a function:

```
>>> x = math.cos(angle + math.pi/2)
```

This statement takes the value of pi, divides it by 2, and adds the result to the value of angle. The sum is then passed as an argument to the cos function.

You can also take the result of one function and pass it as an argument to another:

```
>>> x = math.exp(math.log(10.0))
```

This statement finds the log base e of 10 and then raises e to that power. The result gets assigned to x.

3.6 Adding new functions

So far, we have only been using the functions that come with Python, but it is also possible to add new functions. Creating new functions to solve your particular problems is one of the most useful things about a general-purpose programming language.

In the context of programming, a **function** is a named sequence of statements that performs a desired operation. This operation is specified in a **function definition**. The functions we have been using so far have been defined for us, and these definitions have been hidden. This is a good thing, because it allows us to use the functions without worrying about the details of their definitions.

The syntax for a function definition is:

```
def NAME( LIST OF PARAMETERS ):
  STATEMENTS
```

You can make up any names you want for the functions you create, except that you can't use a name that is a Python keyword. The list of parameters specifies what information, if any, you have to provide in order to use the new function.

There can be any number of statements inside the function, but they have to be indented from the left margin. In the examples in this book, we will use an indentation of two spaces.

The first couple of functions we are going to write have no parameters, so the syntax looks like this:

```
def newLine():
  print
```

This function is named `newLine`. The empty parentheses indicate that it has no parameters. It contains only a single statement, which outputs a newline character. (That's what happens when you use a `print` command without any arguments.)

The syntax for calling the new function is the same as the syntax for built-in functions:

```
print "First Line."
newLine()
print "Second Line."
```

The output of this program is:

```
First line.

Second line.
```

Notice the extra space between the two lines. What if we wanted more space between the lines? We could call the same function repeatedly:

```
print "First Line."
newLine()
newLine()
newLine()
print "Second Line."
```

Or we could write a new function named `threeLines` that prints three new lines:

```
def threeLines():
  newLine()
  newLine()
  newLine()


print "First Line."
threeLines()
print "Second Line."
```

This function contains three statements, all of which are indented by two spaces. Since the next statement is not indented, Python knows that it is not part of the function.

You should notice a few things about this program:

1. You can call the same procedure repeatedly. In fact, it is quite common and useful to do so.

2. You can have one function call another function; in this case `threeLines` calls `newLine`.

So far, it may not be clear why it is worth the trouble to create all of these new functions. Actually, there are a lot of reasons, but this example demonstrates two:

- Creating a new function gives you an opportunity to name a group of statements. Functions can simplify a program by hiding a complex computation behind a single command and by using English words in place of arcane code.

- Creating a new function can make a program smaller by eliminating repetitive code. For example, a short way to print nine consecutive new lines is to call `threeLines` three times.

As an exercise, write a function called `nineLines` *that uses* `threeLines` *to print nine blank lines. How would you print twenty-seven new lines?*

3.7 Definitions and use

Pulling together the code fragments from Section 3.6, the whole program looks like this:

```
def newLine():
  print

def threeLines():
  newLine()
  newLine()
  newLine()

print "First Line."
threeLines()
print "Second Line."
```

This program contains two function definitions: `newLine` and `threeLines`. Function definitions get executed just like other statements, but the effect is to create the new function. The statements inside the function do not get executed until the function is called, and the function definition generates no output.

As you might expect, you have to create a function before you can execute it. In other words, the function definition has to be executed before the first time it is called.

> *As an exercise, move the last three lines of this program to the top, so the function calls appear before the definitions. Run the program and see what error message you get.*

> *As another exercise, start with the working version of the program and move the definition of* `newLine` *after the definition of* `threeLines`*. What happens when you run this program?*

3.8 Flow of execution

In order to ensure that a function is defined before its first use, you have to know the order in which statements are executed, which is called the **flow of execution**.

Execution always begins at the first statement of the program. Statements are executed one at a time, in order from top to bottom.

Function definitions do not alter the flow of execution of the program, but remember that statements inside the function are not executed until the function is called. Although it is not common, you can define one function inside another. In this case, the inner definition isn't executed until the outer function is called.

Function calls are like a detour in the flow of execution. Instead of going to the next statement, the flow jumps to the first line of the called function, executes all the statements there, and then comes back to pick up where it left off.

That sounds simple enough, until you remember that one function can call another. While in the middle of one function, the program might have to execute the statements in another function. But while executing that new function, the program might have to execute yet another function!

Fortunately, Python is adept at keeping track of where it is, so each time a function completes, the program picks up where it left off in the function that called it. When it gets to the end of the program, it terminates.

What's the moral of this sordid tale? When you read a program, don't read from top to bottom. Instead, follow the flow of execution.

3.9 Parameters and arguments

Some of the built-in functions you have used require arguments, the values that control how the function does its job. For example, if you want to find the sine of a number, you have to indicate what the number is. Thus, `sin` takes a numeric value as an argument.

Some functions take more than one argument. For example, `pow` takes two arguments, the base and the exponent. Inside the function, the values that are passed get assigned to variables called **parameters**.

Here is an example of a user-defined function that has a parameter:

```
def printTwice(bruce):
  print bruce, bruce
```

This function takes a single argument and assigns it to a parameter named `bruce`. The value of the parameter (at this point we have no idea what it will be) is printed twice, followed by a newline. The name `bruce` was chosen to suggest that the name you give a parameter is up to you, but in general, you want to choose something more illustrative than `bruce`.

The function `printTwice` works for any type that can be printed:

```
>>> printTwice('Spam')
Spam Spam
```

```
>>> printTwice(5)
5 5
>>> printTwice(3.14159)
3.14159 3.14159
```

In the first function call, the argument is a string. In the second, it's an integer. In the third, it's a `float`.

The same rules of composition that apply to built-in functions also apply to user-defined functions, so we can use any kind of expression as an argument for `printTwice`:

```
>>> printTwice('Spam'*4)
SpamSpamSpamSpam SpamSpamSpamSpam
>>> printTwice(math.cos(math.pi))
-1.0 -1.0
```

As usual, the expression is evaluated before the function is run, so `printTwice` prints `SpamSpamSpamSpam SpamSpamSpamSpam` instead of `'Spam'*4 'Spam'*4`.

> *As an exercise, write a call to* `printTwice` *that does print* `'Spam'*4 'Spam'*4`. *Hint: strings can be enclosed in either single or double quotes, and the type of quote not used to enclose the string can be used inside it as part of the string.*

We can also use a variable as an argument:

```
>>> michael = 'Eric, the half a bee.'
>>> printTwice(michael)
Eric, the half a bee. Eric, the half a bee.
```

Notice something very important here. The name of the variable we pass as an argument (`michael`) has nothing to do with the name of the parameter (`bruce`). It doesn't matter what the value was called back home (in the caller); here in `printTwice`, we call everybody `bruce`.

3.10 Variables and parameters are local

When you create a **local variable** inside a function, it only exists inside the function, and you cannot use it outside. For example:

```
def catTwice(part1, part2):
  cat = part1 + part2
  printTwice(cat)
```

This function takes two arguments, concatenates them, and then prints the result twice. We can call the function with two strings:

```
>>> chant1 = "Pie Jesu domine, "
>>> chant2 = "Dona eis requiem."
>>> catTwice(chant1, chant2)
Pie Jesu domine, Dona eis requiem. Pie Jesu domine, Dona eis requiem.
```

When `catTwice` terminates, the variable `cat` is destroyed. If we try to print it, we get an error:

```
>>> print cat
NameError: cat
```

Parameters are also local. For example, outside the function `printTwice`, there is no such thing as `bruce`. If you try to use it, Python will complain.

3.11 Stack diagrams

To keep track of which variables can be used where, it is sometimes useful to draw a **stack diagram**. Like state diagrams, stack diagrams show the value of each variable, but they also show the function to which each variable belongs.

Each function is represented by a **frame**. A frame is a box with the name of a function beside it and the parameters and variables of the function inside it. The stack diagram for the previous example looks like this:

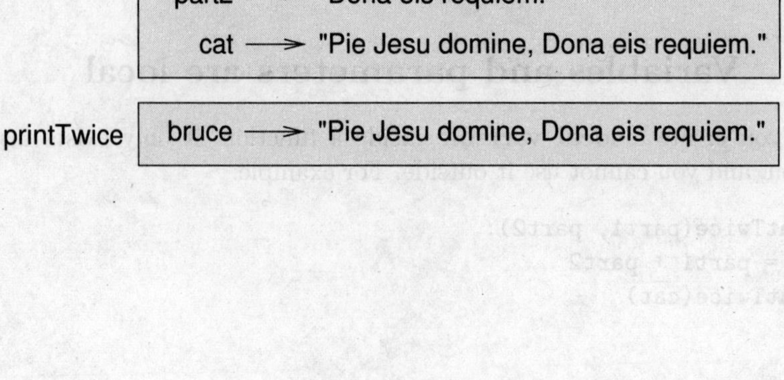

The order of the stack shows the flow of execution. `printTwice` was called by `catTwice`, and `catTwice` was called by `__main__`, which is a special name for the topmost function. When you create a variable outside of any function, it belongs to `__main__`.

Each parameter refers to the same value as its corresponding argument. So, `part1` has the same value as `chant1`, `part2` has the same value as `chant2`, and `bruce` has the same value as `cat`.

If an error occurs during a function call, Python prints the name of the function, and the name of the function that called it, and the name of the function that called *that*, all the way back to `__main__`.

For example, if we try to access `cat` from within `printTwice`, we get a `NameError`:

```
Traceback (innermost last):
  File "test.py", line 13, in __main__
    catTwice(chant1, chant2)
  File "test.py", line 5, in catTwice
    printTwice(cat)
  File "test.py", line 9, in printTwice
    print cat
NameError: cat
```

This list of functions is called a **traceback**. It tells you what program file the error occurred in, and what line, and what functions were executing at the time. It also shows the line of code that caused the error.

Notice the similarity between the traceback and the stack diagram. It's not a coincidence.

3.12 Functions with results

You might have noticed by now that some of the functions we are using, such as the math functions, yield results. Other functions, like `newLine`, perform an action but don't return a value. That raises some questions:

1. What happens if you call a function and you don't do anything with the result (i.e., you don't assign it to a variable or use it as part of a larger expression)?

2. What happens if you use a function without a result as part of an expression, such as `newLine() + 7`?

3. Can you write functions that yield results, or are you stuck with simple function like `newLine` and `printTwice`?

The answer to the last question is that you can write functions that yield results, and we'll do it in Chapter 5.

> *As an exercise, answer the other two questions by trying them out. When you have a question about what is legal or illegal in Python, a good way to find out is to ask the interpreter.*

3.13 Glossary

function call: A statement that executes a function. It consists of the name of the function followed by a list of arguments enclosed in parentheses.

argument: A value provided to a function when the function is called. This value is assigned to the corresponding parameter in the function.

return value: The result of a function. If a function call is used as an expression, the return value is the value of the expression.

type conversion: An explicit statement that takes a value of one type and computes a corresponding value of another type.

type coercion: A type conversion that happens automatically according to Python's coercion rules.

module: A file that contains a collection of related functions and classes.

dot notation: The syntax for calling a function in another module, specifying the module name followed by a dot (period) and the function name.

function: A named sequence of statements that performs some useful operation. Functions may or may not take arguments and may or may not produce a result.

function definition: A statement that creates a new function, specifying its name, parameters, and the statements it executes.

flow of execution: The order in which statements are executed during a program run.

parameter: A name used inside a function to refer to the value passed as an argument.

local variable: A variable defined inside a function. A local variable can only be used inside its function.

stack diagram: A graphical representation of a stack of functions, their variables, and the values to which they refer.

frame: A box in a stack diagram that represents a function call. It contains the local variables and parameters of the function.

traceback: A list of the functions that are executing, printed when a runtime error occurs.

Chapter 4

Conditionals and recursion

4.1 The modulus operator

The **modulus operator** works on integers (and integer expressions) and yields the remainder when the first operand is divided by the second. In Python, the modulus operator is a percent sign (`%`). The syntax is the same as for other operators:

```
>>> quotient = 7 / 3
>>> print quotient
2
>>> remainder = 7 % 3
>>> print remainder
1
```

So 7 divided by 3 is 2 with 1 left over.

The modulus operator turns out to be surprisingly useful. For example, you can check whether one number is divisible by another—if `x % y` is zero, then `x` is divisible by `y`.

Also, you can extract the right-most digit or digits from a number. For example, `x % 10` yields the right-most digit of `x` (in base 10). Similarly `x % 100` yields the last two digits.

4.2 Boolean expressions

A **boolean expression** is an expression that is either true or false. One way to write a boolean expression is to use the operator `==`, which compares two values and produces a boolean value:

```
>>> 5 == 5
True
>>> 5 == 6
False
```

In the first statement, the two operands are equal, so the value of the expression is `True`; in the second statement, 5 is not equal to 6, so we get `False`. `True` and `False` are special values that are built into Python.

The `==` operator is one of the **comparison operators**; the others are:

```
x != y          # x is not equal to y
x > y           # x is greater than y
x < y           # x is less than y
x >= y          # x is greater than or equal to y
x <= y          # x is less than or equal to y
```

Although these operations are probably familiar to you, the Python symbols are different from the mathematical symbols. A common error is to use a single equal sign (`=`) instead of a double equal sign (`==`). Remember that `=` is an assignment operator and `==` is a comparison operator. Also, there is no such thing as `=<` or `=>`.

4.3 Logical operators

There are three **logical operators**: `and`, `or`, and `not`. The semantics (meaning) of these operators is similar to their meaning in English. For example, `x > 0 and x < 10` is true only if `x` is greater than 0 *and* less than 10.

`n%2 == 0 or n%3 == 0` is true if *either* of the conditions is true, that is, if the number is divisible by 2 *or* 3.

Finally, the `not` operator negates a boolean expression, so `not(x > y)` is true if `(x > y)` is false, that is, if `x` is less than or equal to `y`.

Strictly speaking, the operands of the logical operators should be boolean expressions, but Python is not very strict. Any nonzero number is interpreted as "true."

```
>>>  x = 5
>>>  x and 1
1
>>>  y = 0
>>>  y and 1
0
```

In general, this sort of thing is not considered good style. If you want to compare a value to zero, you should do it explicitly.

4.4 Conditional execution

In order to write useful programs, we almost always need the ability to check conditions and change the behavior of the program accordingly. **Conditional statements** give us this ability. The simplest form is the `if` statement:

```
if x > 0:
  print "x is positive"
```

The boolean expression after the `if` statement is called the **condition**. If it is true, then the indented statement gets executed. If not, nothing happens.

Like other compound statements, the `if` statement is made up of a header and a block of statements:

```
HEADER:
  FIRST STATEMENT
  ...
  LAST STATEMENT
```

The header begins on a new line and ends with a colon (:). The indented statements that follow are called a **block**. The first unindented statement marks the end of the block. A statement block inside a compound statement is called the **body** of the statement.

There is no limit on the number of statements that can appear in the body of an if statement, but there has to be at least one. Occasionally, it is useful to have a body with no statements (usually as a place keeper for code you haven't written yet). In that case, you can use the `pass` statement, which does nothing.

4.5 Alternative execution

A second form of the `if` statement is alternative execution, in which there are two possibilities and the condition determines which one gets executed. The syntax looks like this:

```
if x%2 == 0:
  print x, "is even"
else:
  print x, "is odd"
```

If the remainder when x is divided by 2 is 0, then we know that x is even, and the program displays a message to that effect. If the condition is false, the second set of statements is executed. Since the condition must be true or false, exactly one of the alternatives will be executed. The alternatives are called **branches**, because they are branches in the flow of execution.

As an aside, if you need to check the parity (evenness or oddness) of numbers often, you might "wrap" this code in a function:

```
def printParity(x):
  if x%2 == 0:
    print x, "is even"
  else:
    print x, "is odd"
```

For any value of x, printParity displays an appropriate message. When you call it, you can provide any integer expression as an argument.

```
>>> printParity(17)
17 is odd
>>> y = 17
>>> printParity(y+1)
18 is even
```

4.6 Chained conditionals

Sometimes there are more than two possibilities and we need more than two branches. One way to express a computation like that is a **chained conditional**:

```
if x < y:
  print x, "is less than", y
elif x > y:
  print x, "is greater than", y
else:
  print x, "and", y, "are equal"
```

elif is an abbreviation of "else if." Again, exactly one branch will be executed. There is no limit of the number of elif statements, but the last branch has to be an else statement:

```
if choice == 'A':
  functionA()
elif choice == 'B':
  functionB()
elif choice == 'C':
  functionC()
else:
  print "Invalid choice."
```

Each condition is checked in order. If the first is false, the next is checked, and so on. If one of them is true, the corresponding branch executes, and the statement ends. Even if more than one condition is true, only the first true branch executes.

> *As an exercise, wrap these examples in functions called* `compare(x, y)` *and* `dispatch(choice)`.

4.7 Nested conditionals

One conditional can also be nested within another. We could have written the trichotomy example as follows:

```
if x == y:
  print x, "and", y, "are equal"
else:
  if x < y:
    print x, "is less than", y
  else:
    print x, "is greater than", y
```

The outer conditional contains two branches. The first branch contains a simple output statement. The second branch contains another `if` statement, which has two branches of its own. Those two branches are both output statements, although they could have been conditional statements as well.

Although the indentation of the statements makes the structure apparent, nested conditionals become difficult to read very quickly. In general, it is a good idea to avoid them when you can.

Logical operators often provide a way to simplify nested conditional statements. For example, we can rewrite the following code using a single conditional:

```
if 0 < x:
  if x < 10:
    print "x is a positive single digit."
```

The `print` statement is executed only if we make it past both the conditionals, so we can use the `and` operator:

```
if 0 < x and x < 10:
  print "x is a positive single digit."
```

These kinds of conditions are common, so Python provides an alternative syntax that is similar to mathematical notation:

```
if 0 < x < 10:
  print "x is a positive single digit."
```

This condition is semantically the same as the compound boolean expression and the nested conditional.

4.8 The return statement

The `return` statement allows you to terminate the execution of a function before you reach the end. One reason to use it is if you detect an error condition:

```
import math

def printLogarithm(x):
  if x <= 0:
    print "Positive numbers only, please."
    return

  result = math.log(x)
  print "The log of x is", result
```

The function `printLogarithm` has a parameter named `x`. The first thing it does is check whether `x` is less than or equal to 0, in which case it displays an error message and then uses `return` to exit the function. The flow of execution immediately returns to the caller, and the remaining lines of the function are not executed.

Remember that to use a function from the math module, you have to import it.

4.9 Recursion

We mentioned that it is legal for one function to call another, and you have seen several examples of that. We neglected to mention that it is also legal for a function to call itself. It may not be obvious why that is a good thing, but it turns out to be one of the most magical and interesting things a program can do. For example, look at the following function:

```
def countdown(n):
  if n == 0:
    print "Blastoff!"
  else:
    print n
    countdown(n-1)
```

`countdown` expects the parameter, `n`, to be a positive integer. If `n` is 0, it outputs the word, "Blastoff!" Otherwise, it outputs `n` and then calls a function named `countdown`—itself—passing `n-1` as an argument.

What happens if we call this function like this:

```
>>> countdown(3)
```

The execution of `countdown` begins with `n=3`, and since `n` is not 0, it outputs the value 3, and then calls itself...

> The execution of `countdown` begins with `n=2`, and since `n` is not 0, it outputs the value 2, and then calls itself...
>
> > The execution of `countdown` begins with `n=1`, and since `n` is not 0, it outputs the value 1, and then calls itself...
> >
> > > The execution of `countdown` begins with `n=0`, and since `n` is 0, it outputs the word, "Blastoff!" and then returns.
> >
> > The `countdown` that got `n=1` returns.
>
> The `countdown` that got `n=2` returns.

The `countdown` that got `n=3` returns.

And then you're back in `__main__` (what a trip). So, the total output looks like this:

```
3
2
1
Blastoff!
```

As a second example, look again at the functions `newLine` and `threeLines`:

```
def newline():
  print

def threeLines():
  newLine()
  newLine()
  newLine()
```

Although these work, they would not be much help if we wanted to output 2 newlines, or 106. A better alternative would be this:

```
def nLines(n):
  if n > 0:
    print
    nLines(n-1)
```

This program is similar to `countdown`; as long as `n` is greater than 0, it outputs one newline and then calls itself to output `n-1` additional newlines. Thus, the total number of newlines is `1 + (n - 1)` which, if you do your algebra right, comes out to `n`.

The process of a function calling itself is **recursion**, and such functions are said to be recursive.

4.10 Stack diagrams for recursive functions

In Section 3.11, we used a stack diagram to represent the state of a program during a function call. The same kind of diagram can help interpret a recursive function.

Every time a function gets called, Python creates a new function frame, which contains the function's local variables and parameters. For a recursive function, there might be more than one frame on the stack at the same time.

This figure shows a stack diagram for `countdown` called with `n = 3`:

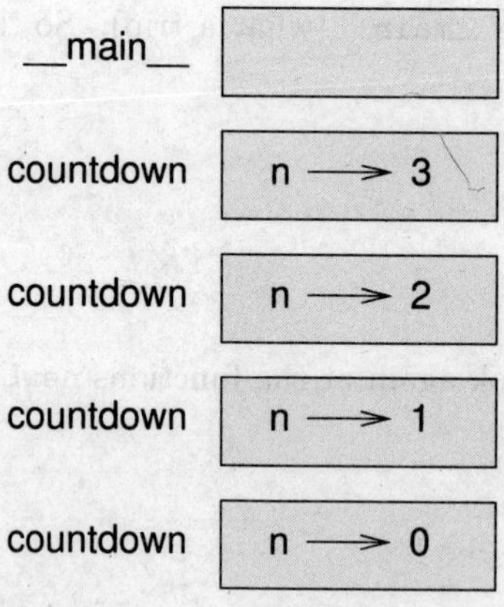

As usual, the top of the stack is the frame for `__main__`. It is empty because we did not create any variables in `__main__` or pass any arguments to it.

The four `countdown` frames have different values for the parameter `n`. The bottom of the stack, where `n=0`, is called the **base case**. It does not make a recursive call, so there are no more frames.

As an exercise, draw a stack diagram for `nLines` *called with* `n=4`.

4.11 Infinite recursion

If a recursion never reaches a base case, it goes on making recursive calls forever, and the program never terminates. This is known as **infinite recursion**, and it is generally not considered a good idea. Here is a minimal program with an infinite recursion:

```
def recurse():
  recurse()
```

In most programming environments, a program with infinite recursion does not really run forever. Python reports an error message when the maximum recursion depth is reached:

```
  File "<stdin>", line 2, in recurse
  (98 repetitions omitted)
  File "<stdin>", line 2, in recurse
RuntimeError: Maximum recursion depth exceeded
```

This traceback is a little bigger than the one we saw in the previous chapter. When the error occurs, there are 100 `recurse` frames on the stack!

> *As an exercise, write a function with infinite recursion and run it in the Python interpreter.*

4.12 Keyboard input

The programs we have written so far are a bit rude in the sense that they accept no input from the user. They just do the same thing every time.

Python provides built-in functions that get input from the keyboard. The simplest is called `raw_input`. When this function is called, the program stops and waits for the user to type something. When the user presses Return or the Enter key, the program resumes and `raw_input` returns what the user typed as a **string**:

```
>>> input = raw_input ()
What are you waiting for?
>>> print input
What are you waiting for?
```

Before calling `raw_input`, it is a good idea to print a message telling the user what to input. This message is called a **prompt**. We can supply a prompt as an argument to `raw_input`:

```
>>> name = raw_input ("What...is your name? ")
What...is your name? Arthur, King of the Britons!
>>> print name
Arthur, King of the Britons!
```

If we expect the response to be an integer, we can use the `input` function:

```
prompt = "What...is the airspeed velocity of an unladen swallow?\n"
speed = input(prompt)
```

The sequence `\n` at the end of the string represents a newline, so the user's input appears below the prompt.

If the user types a string of digits, it is converted to an integer and assigned to `speed`. Unfortunately, if the user types a character that is not a digit, the program crashes:

```
>>> speed = input (prompt)
What...is the airspeed velocity of an unladen swallow?
What do you mean, an African or a European swallow?
SyntaxError: invalid syntax
```

To avoid this kind of error, it is generally a good idea to use `raw_input` to get a string and then use conversion functions to convert to other types.

4.13 Glossary

modulus operator: An operator, denoted with a percent sign (`%`), that works on integers and yields the remainder when one number is divided by another.

boolean expression: An expression that is either true or false.

comparison operator: One of the operators that compares two values: `==`, `!=`, `>`, `<`, `>=`, and `<=`.

logical operator: One of the operators that combines boolean expressions: `and`, `or`, and `not`.

conditional statement: A statement that controls the flow of execution depending on some condition.

condition: The boolean expression in a conditional statement that determines which branch is executed.

compound statement: A statement that consists of a header and a body. The header ends with a colon (:). The body is indented relative to the header.

block: A group of consecutive statements with the same indentation.

body: The block in a compound statement that follows the header.

nesting: One program structure within another, such as a conditional statement inside a branch of another conditional statement.

recursion: The process of calling the function that is currently executing.

base case: A branch of the conditional statement in a recursive function that does not result in a recursive call.

infinite recursion: A function that calls itself recursively without ever reaching the base case. Eventually, an infinite recursion causes a runtime error.

prompt: A visual cue that tells the user to input data.

block: A group of consecutive statements with the same indentation.

body: The block in a compound statement that follows the header.

nesting: One program structure within another, such as a conditional statement inside a branch of another conditional statement.

recursion: The process of calling the function that is currently executing.

base case: A branch of the conditional statement in a recursive function that does not result in a recursive call.

infinite recursion: A function that calls itself recursively without ever reaching the base case. Eventually, an infinite recursion causes a runtime error.

prompt: A visual cue that tells the user to input data.

Chapter 5

Fruitful functions

5.1 Return values

Some of the built-in functions we have used, such as the math functions, have produced results. Calling the function generates a new value, which we usually assign to a variable or use as part of an expression.

```
e = math.exp(1.0)
height = radius * math.sin(angle)
```

But so far, none of the functions we have written has returned a value.

In this chapter, we are going to write functions that return values, which we will call **fruitful functions**, for want of a better name. The first example is `area`, which returns the area of a circle with the given radius:

```
import math

def area(radius):
  temp = math.pi * radius**2
  return temp
```

We have seen the `return` statement before, but in a fruitful function the `return` statement includes a **return value**. This statement means: "Return immediately from this function and use the following expression as a return value." The expression provided can be arbitrarily complicated, so we could have written this function more concisely:

```
def area(radius):
  return math.pi * radius**2
```

On the other hand, **temporary variables** like `temp` often make debugging easier.

Sometimes it is useful to have multiple return statements, one in each branch of a conditional:

```
def absoluteValue(x):
  if x < 0:
    return -x
  else:
    return x
```

Since these `return` statements are in an alternative conditional, only one will be executed. As soon as one is executed, the function terminates without executing any subsequent statements.

Code that appears after a `return` statement, or any other place the flow of execution can never reach, is called **dead code**.

In a fruitful function, it is a good idea to ensure that every possible path through the program hits a `return` statement. For example:

```
def absoluteValue(x):
  if x < 0:
    return -x
  elif x > 0:
    return x
```

This program is not correct because if `x` happens to be 0, neither condition is true, and the function ends without hitting a `return` statement. In this case, the return value is a special value called `None`:

```
>>> print absoluteValue(0)
None
```

> *As an exercise, write a* `compare` *function that returns* `1` *if* `x > y`, `0` *if* `x == y`, *and* `-1` *if* `x < y`.

5.2 Program development

At this point, you should be able to look at complete functions and tell what they do. Also, if you have been doing the exercises, you have written some small functions. As you write larger functions, you might start to have more difficulty, especially with runtime and semantic errors.

To deal with increasingly complex programs, we are going to suggest a technique called **incremental development**. The goal of incremental development is to avoid long debugging sessions by adding and testing only a small amount of code at a time.

As an example, suppose you want to find the distance between two points, given by the coordinates (x_1, y_1) and (x_2, y_2). By the Pythagorean theorem, the distance is:

$$\text{distance} = \sqrt{(x_2 - x_1)^2 + (y_2 - y_1)^2}$$

The first step is to consider what a `distance` function should look like in Python. In other words, what are the inputs (parameters) and what is the output (return value)?

In this case, the two points are the inputs, which we can represent using four parameters. The return value is the distance, which is a floating-point value.

Already we can write an outline of the function:

```
def distance(x1, y1, x2, y2):
  return 0.0
```

Obviously, this version of the function doesn't compute distances; it always returns zero. But it is syntactically correct, and it will run, which means that we can test it before we make it more complicated.

To test the new function, we call it with sample values:

```
>>> distance(1, 2, 4, 6)
0.0
```

We chose these values so that the horizontal distance equals 3 and the vertical distance equals 4; that way, the result is 5 (the hypotenuse of a 3-4-5 triangle). When testing a function, it is useful to know the right answer.

At this point we have confirmed that the function is syntactically correct, and we can start adding lines of code. After each incremental change, we test the function again. If an error occurs at any point, we know where it must be—in the last line we added.

A logical first step in the computation is to find the differences $x_2 - x_1$ and $y_2 - y_1$. We will store those values in temporary variables named `dx` and `dy` and print them.

```
def distance(x1, y1, x2, y2):
  dx = x2 - x1
  dy = y2 - y1
  print "dx is", dx
  print "dy is", dy
  return 0.0
```

If the function is working, the outputs should be 3 and 4. If so, we know that the function is getting the right arguments and performing the first computation correctly. If not, there are only a few lines to check.

Next we compute the sum of squares of dx and dy:

```
def distance(x1, y1, x2, y2):
  dx = x2 - x1
  dy = y2 - y1
  dsquared = dx**2 + dy**2
  print "dsquared is: ", dsquared
  return 0.0
```

Notice that we removed the `print` statements we wrote in the previous step. Code like that is called **scaffolding** because it is helpful for building the program but is not part of the final product.

Again, we would run the program at this stage and check the output (which should be 25).

Finally, if we have imported the math module, we can use the `sqrt` function to compute and return the result:

```
def distance(x1, y1, x2, y2):
  dx = x2 - x1
  dy = y2 - y1
  dsquared = dx**2 + dy**2
  result = math.sqrt(dsquared)
  return result
```

If that works correctly, you are done. Otherwise, you might want to print the value of `result` before the return statement.

When you start out, you should add only a line or two of code at a time. As you gain more experience, you might find yourself writing and debugging bigger chunks. Either way, the incremental development process can save you a lot of debugging time.

The key aspects of the process are:

1. Start with a working program and make small incremental changes. At any point, if there is an error, you will know exactly where it is.

2. Use temporary variables to hold intermediate values so you can output and check them.

3. Once the program is working, you might want to remove some of the scaffolding or consolidate multiple statements into compound expressions, but only if it does not make the program difficult to read.

   As an exercise, use incremental development to write a function called `hypotenuse` *that returns the length of the hypotenuse of a right triangle given the lengths of the two legs as arguments. Record each stage of the incremental development process as you go.*

5.3 Composition

As you should expect by now, you can call one function from within another. This ability is called **composition**.

As an example, we'll write a function that takes two points, the center of the circle and a point on the perimeter, and computes the area of the circle.

Assume that the center point is stored in the variables `xc` and `yc`, and the perimeter point is in `xp` and `yp`. The first step is to find the radius of the circle, which is the distance between the two points. Fortunately, there is a function, `distance`, that does that:

```
radius = distance(xc, yc, xp, yp)
```

The second step is to find the area of a circle with that radius and return it:

```
result = area(radius)
return result
```

Wrapping that up in a function, we get:

```
def area2(xc, yc, xp, yp):
  radius = distance(xc, yc, xp, yp)
  result = area(radius)
  return result
```

We called this function `area2` to distinguish it from the `area` function defined earlier. There can only be one function with a given name within a given module.

The temporary variables `radius` and `result` are useful for development and debugging, but once the program is working, we can make it more concise by composing the function calls:

```
def area2(xc, yc, xp, yp):
  return area(distance(xc, yc, xp, yp))
```

As an exercise, write a function `slope(x1, y1, x2, y2)` *that returns the slope of the line through the points* $(x1, y1)$ *and* $(x2, y2)$*. Then use this function in a function called* `intercept(x1, y1, x2, y2)` *that returns the y-intercept of the line through the points* `(x1, y1)` *and* `(x2, y2)`.

5.4 Boolean functions

Functions can return boolean values, which is often convenient for hiding complicated tests inside functions. For example:

```
def isDivisible(x, y):
  if x % y == 0:
    return True
  else:
    return False
```

The name of this function is `isDivisible`. It is common to give boolean functions names that sound like yes/no questions. `isDivisible` returns either `True` or `False` to indicate whether the `x` is or is not divisible by `y`.

We can make the function more concise by taking advantage of the fact that the condition of the `if` statement is itself a boolean expression. We can return it directly, avoiding the `if` statement altogether:

```
def isDivisible(x, y):
  return x % y == 0
```

This session shows the new function in action:

```
>>>   isDivisible(6, 4)
False
>>>   isDivisible(6, 3)
True
```

Boolean functions are often used in conditional statements:

```
if isDivisible(x, y):
  print "x is divisible by y"
else:
  print "x is not divisible by y"
```

It might be tempting to write something like:

```
if isDivisible(x, y) == True:
```

But the extra comparison is unnecessary.

> *As an exercise, write a function* `isBetween(x, y, z)` *that returns* `True` *if* $y \leq x \leq z$ *or* `False` *otherwise.*

5.5 More recursion

So far, you have only learned a small subset of Python, but you might be interested to know that this subset is a *complete* programming language, which means that anything that can be computed can be expressed in this language. Any program ever written could be rewritten using only the language features you have learned so far (actually, you would need a few commands to control devices like the keyboard, mouse, disks, etc., but that's all).

Proving that claim is a nontrivial exercise first accomplished by Alan Turing, one of the first computer scientists (some would argue that he was a mathematician, but a lot of early computer scientists started as mathematicians). Accordingly, it is known as the Turing Thesis. If you take a course on the Theory of Computation, you will have a chance to see the proof.

To give you an idea of what you can do with the tools you have learned so far, we'll evaluate a few recursively defined mathematical functions. A recursive definition is similar to a circular definition, in the sense that the definition contains a reference to the thing being defined. A truly circular definition is not very useful:

frabjuous: An adjective used to describe something that is frabjuous.

If you saw that definition in the dictionary, you might be annoyed. On the other hand, if you looked up the definition of the mathematical function factorial, you might get something like this:

$$0! = 1$$

$$n! = n(n-1)!$$

This definition says that the factorial of 0 is 1, and the factorial of any other value, n, is n multiplied by the factorial of $n-1$.

So 3! is 3 times 2!, which is 2 times 1!, which is 1 times 0!. Putting it all together, 3! equals 3 times 2 times 1 times 1, which is 6.

If you can write a recursive definition of something, you can usually write a Python program to evaluate it. The first step is to decide what the parameters are for this function. With little effort, you should conclude that `factorial` has a single parameter:

```
def factorial(n):
```

If the argument happens to be 0, all we have to do is return 1:

```
def factorial(n):
  if n == 0:
    return 1
```

Otherwise, and this is the interesting part, we have to make a recursive call to find the factorial of $n-1$ and then multiply it by n:

```
def factorial(n):
  if n == 0:
    return 1
  else:
    recurse = factorial(n-1)
    result = n * recurse
    return result
```

The flow of execution for this program is similar to the flow of `countdown` in Section 4.9. If we call `factorial` with the value 3:

Since 3 is not 0, we take the second branch and calculate the factorial of `n-1`...

> Since 2 is not 0, we take the second branch and calculate the factorial of `n-1`...
>
> > Since 1 is not 0, we take the second branch and calculate the factorial of `n-1`...
> >
> > > Since 0 *is* 0, we take the first branch and return 1 without making any more recursive calls.
> >
> > The return value (1) is multiplied by n, which is 1, and the result is returned.
>
> The return value (1) is multiplied by n, which is 2, and the result is returned.

The return value (2) is multiplied by n, which is 3, and the result, 6, becomes the return value of the function call that started the whole process.

Here is what the stack diagram looks like for this sequence of function calls:

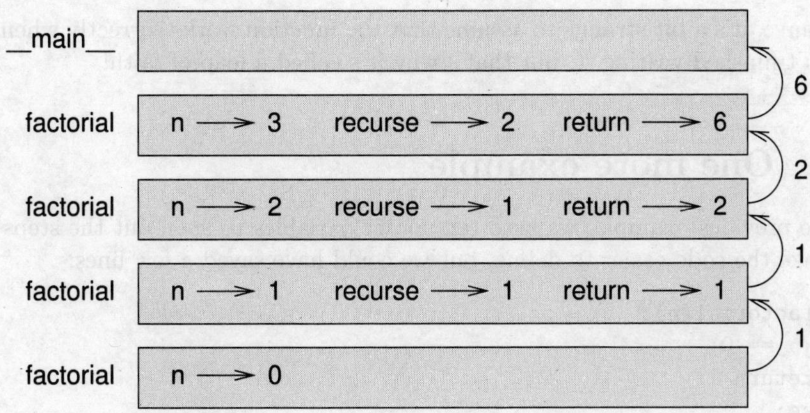

The return values are shown being passed back up the stack. In each frame, the return value is the value of `result`, which is the product of `n` and `recurse`.

Notice that in the last frame, the local variables `recurse` and `result` do not exist, because the branch that creates them did not execute.

5.6 Leap of faith

Following the flow of execution is one way to read programs, but it can quickly become labyrinthine. An alternative is what we call the "leap of faith." When you come to a function call, instead of following the flow of execution, you *assume* that the function works correctly and returns the appropriate value.

In fact, you are already practicing this leap of faith when you use built-in functions. When you call `math.cos` or `math.exp`, you don't examine the implementations of those functions. You just assume that they work because the people who wrote the built-in functions were good programmers.

The same is true when you call one of your own functions. For example, in Section 5.4, we wrote a function called `isDivisible` that determines whether one number is divisible by another. Once we have convinced ourselves that this function is correct—by testing and examining the code—we can use the function without looking at the code again.

The same is true of recursive programs. When you get to the recursive call, instead of following the flow of execution, you should assume that the recursive call works (yields the correct result) and then ask yourself, "Assuming that I can find the factorial of $n - 1$, can I compute the factorial of n?" In this case, it is clear that you can, by multiplying by n.

Of course, it's a bit strange to assume that the function works correctly when you haven't finished writing it, but that's why it's called a leap of faith!

5.7 One more example

In the previous example, we used temporary variables to spell out the steps and to make the code easier to debug, but we could have saved a few lines:

```
def factorial(n):
    if n == 0:
        return 1
    else:
        return n * factorial(n-1)
```

From now on, we will tend to use the more concise form, but we recommend that you use the more explicit version while you are developing code. When you have it working, you can tighten it up if you are feeling inspired.

After `factorial`, the most common example of a recursively defined mathematical function is `fibonacci`, which has the following definition:

$$\text{fibonacci}(0) = 1$$

$$\text{fibonacci}(1) = 1$$

$$\text{fibonacci}(n) = \text{fibonacci}(n-1) + \text{fibonacci}(n-2);$$

Translated into Python, it looks like this:

```
def fibonacci (n):
    if n == 0 or n == 1:
        return 1
    else:
        return fibonacci(n-1) + fibonacci(n-2)
```

If you try to follow the flow of execution here, even for fairly small values of n, your head explodes. But according to the leap of faith, if you assume that the two recursive calls work correctly, then it is clear that you get the right result by adding them together.

5.8 Checking types

What happens if we call `factorial` and give it 1.5 as an argument?

```
>>> factorial (1.5)
RuntimeError: Maximum recursion depth exceeded
```

It looks like an infinite recursion. But how can that be? There is a base case—when `n == 0`. The problem is that the values of `n` *miss* the base case.

In the first recursive call, the value of `n` is 0.5. In the next, it is -0.5. From there, it gets smaller and smaller, but it will never be 0.

We have two choices. We can try to generalize the `factorial` function to work with floating-point numbers, or we can make `factorial` check the type of its argument. The first option is called the gamma function and it's a little beyond the scope of this book. So we'll go for the second.

We can use the built-in function `isinstance` to verify the type of the argument. While we're at it, we also make sure the argument is positive:

```
def factorial (n):
  if not isinstance(n, int):
    print "Factorial is only defined for integers."
    return -1
  elif n < 0:
    print "Factorial is only defined for positive integers."
    return -1
  elif n == 0:
    return 1
  else:
    return n * factorial(n-1)
```

Now we have three base cases. The first catches nonintegers. The second catches negative integers. In both cases, the program prints an error message and returns a special value, -1, to indicate that something went wrong:

```
>>> factorial ("fred")
Factorial is only defined for integers.
-1
>>> factorial (-2)
Factorial is only defined for positive integers.
-1
```

If we get past both checks, then we know that n is a positive integer, and we can prove that the recursion terminates.

This program demonstrates a pattern sometimes called a **guardian**. The first two conditionals act as guardians, protecting the code that follows from values that might cause an error. The guardians make it possible to prove the correctness of the code.

5.9 Glossary

fruitful function: A function that yields a return value.

return value: The value provided as the result of a function call.

temporary variable: A variable used to store an intermediate value in a complex calculation.

dead code: Part of a program that can never be executed, often because it appears after a `return` statement.

`None`**:** A special Python value returned by functions that have no return statement, or a return statement without an argument.

incremental development: A program development plan intended to avoid debugging by adding and testing only a small amount of code at a time.

scaffolding: Code that is used during program development but is not part of the final version.

guardian: A condition that checks for and handles circumstances that might cause an error.

Chapter 6

Iteration

6.1 Multiple assignment

As you may have discovered, it is legal to make more than one assignment to the same variable. A new assignment makes an existing variable refer to a new value (and stop referring to the old value).

```
bruce = 5
print bruce,
bruce = 7
print bruce
```

The output of this program is `5 7`, because the first time `bruce` is printed, his value is 5, and the second time, his value is 7. The comma at the end of the first `print` statement suppresses the newline after the output, which is why both outputs appear on the same line.

Here is what **multiple assignment** looks like in a state diagram:

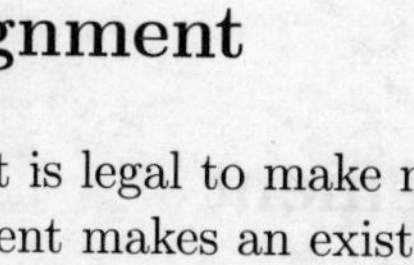

With multiple assignment it is especially important to distinguish between an assignment operation and a statement of equality. Because Python uses the equal sign (=) for assignment, it is tempting to interpret a statement like `a = b` as a statement of equality. It is not!

First, equality is commutative and assignment is not. For example, in mathematics, if $a = 7$ then $7 = a$. But in Python, the statement `a = 7` is legal and `7 = a` is not.

Furthermore, in mathematics, a statement of equality is always true. If $a = b$ now, then a will always equal b. In Python, an assignment statement can make two variables equal, but they don't have to stay that way:

```
a = 5
b = a    # a and b are now equal
a = 3    # a and b are no longer equal
```

The third line changes the value of `a` but does not change the value of `b`, so they are no longer equal. (In some programming languages, a different symbol is used for assignment, such as `<-` or `:=`, to avoid confusion.)

Although multiple assignment is frequently helpful, you should use it with caution. If the values of variables change frequently, it can make the code difficult to read and debug.

6.2 The `while` statement

Computers are often used to automate repetitive tasks. Repeating identical or similar tasks without making errors is something that computers do well and people do poorly.

We have seen two programs, `nLines` and `countdown`, that use recursion to perform repetition, which is also called **iteration**. Because iteration is so common, Python provides several language features to make it easier. The first feature we are going to look at is the `while` statement.

Here is what `countdown` looks like with a `while` statement:

```
def countdown(n):
  while n > 0:
    print n
    n = n-1
  print "Blastoff!"
```

Since we removed the recursive call, this function is not recursive.

You can almost read the `while` statement as if it were English. It means, "While `n` is greater than 0, continue displaying the value of `n` and then reducing the value of `n` by 1. When you get to 0, display the word `Blastoff!`"

More formally, here is the flow of execution for a `while` statement:

1. Evaluate the condition, yielding 0 or 1.
2. If the condition is false (0), exit the `while` statement and continue execution at the next statement.
3. If the condition is true (1), execute each of the statements in the body and then go back to step 1.

The body consists of all of the statements below the header with the same indentation.

This type of flow is called a **loop** because the third step loops back around to the top. Notice that if the condition is false the first time through the loop, the statements inside the loop are never executed.

The body of the loop should change the value of one or more variables so that eventually the condition becomes false and the loop terminates. Otherwise the loop will repeat forever, which is called an **infinite loop**. An endless source of amusement for computer scientists is the observation that the directions on shampoo, "Lather, rinse, repeat," are an infinite loop.

In the case of `countdown`, we can prove that the loop terminates because we know that the value of `n` is finite, and we can see that the value of `n` gets smaller each time through the loop, so eventually we have to get to 0. In other cases, it is not so easy to tell:

```
def sequence(n):
  while n != 1:
    print n,
    if n%2 == 0:            # n is even
      n = n/2
    else:                   # n is odd
      n = n*3+1
```

The condition for this loop is `n != 1`, so the loop will continue until `n` is 1, which will make the condition false.

Each time through the loop, the program outputs the value of `n` and then checks whether it is even or odd. If it is even, the value of `n` is divided by 2. If it is odd, the value is replaced by `n*3+1`. For example, if the starting value (the argument passed to `sequence`) is 3, the resulting sequence is 3, 10, 5, 16, 8, 4, 2, 1.

Since `n` sometimes increases and sometimes decreases, there is no obvious proof that `n` will ever reach 1, or that the program terminates. For some particular values of `n`, we can prove termination. For example, if the starting value is a power of two, then the value of `n` will be even each time through the loop until it reaches 1. The previous example ends with such a sequence, starting with 16.

Particular values aside, the interesting question is whether we can prove that this program terminates for *all positive values* of n. So far, no one has been able to prove it *or* disprove it!

> *As an exercise, rewrite the function* nLines *from Section 4.9 using iteration instead of recursion.*

6.3 Tables

One of the things loops are good for is generating tabular data. Before computers were readily available, people had to calculate logarithms, sines and cosines, and other mathematical functions by hand. To make that easier, mathematics books contained long tables listing the values of these functions. Creating the tables was slow and boring, and they tended to be full of errors.

When computers appeared on the scene, one of the initial reactions was, "This is great! We can use the computers to generate the tables, so there will be no errors." That turned out to be true (mostly) but shortsighted. Soon thereafter, computers and calculators were so pervasive that the tables became obsolete.

Well, almost. For some operations, computers use tables of values to get an approximate answer and then perform computations to improve the approximation. In some cases, there have been errors in the underlying tables, most famously in the table the Intel Pentium used to perform floating-point division.

Although a log table is not as useful as it once was, it still makes a good example of iteration. The following program outputs a sequence of values in the left column and their logarithms in the right column:

```
x = 1.0
while x < 10.0:
  print x, '\t', math.log(x)
  x = x + 1.0
```

The string '\t' represents a **tab** character.

As characters and strings are displayed on the screen, an invisible marker called the **cursor** keeps track of where the next character will go. After a print statement, the cursor normally goes to the beginning of the next line.

The tab character shifts the cursor to the right until it reaches one of the tab stops. Tabs are useful for making columns of text line up, as in the output of the previous program:

```
1.0     0.0
2.0     0.69314718056
3.0     1.09861228867
4.0     1.38629436112
5.0     1.60943791243
6.0     1.79175946923
7.0     1.94591014906
8.0     2.07944154168
9.0     2.19722457734
```

If these values seem odd, remember that the `log` function uses base `e`. Since powers of two are so important in computer science, we often want to find logarithms with respect to base 2. To do that, we can use the following formula:

$$\log_2 x = \frac{\log_e x}{\log_e 2}$$

Changing the output statement to:

```
print x, '\t',  math.log(x)/math.log(2.0)
```

yields:

```
1.0     0.0
2.0     1.0
3.0     1.58496250072
4.0     2.0
5.0     2.32192809489
6.0     2.58496250072
7.0     2.80735492206
8.0     3.0
9.0     3.16992500144
```

We can see that 1, 2, 4, and 8 are powers of two because their logarithms base 2 are round numbers. If we wanted to find the logarithms of other powers of two, we could modify the program like this:

```
x = 1.0
while x < 100.0:
  print x, '\t', math.log(x)/math.log(2.0)
  x = x * 2.0
```

Now instead of adding something to `x` each time through the loop, which yields an arithmetic sequence, we multiply `x` by something, yielding a geometric sequence. The result is:

```
1.0     0.0
2.0     1.0
4.0     2.0
8.0     3.0
16.0    4.0
32.0    5.0
64.0    6.0
```

Because of the tab characters between the columns, the position of the second column does not depend on the number of digits in the first column.

Logarithm tables may not be useful any more, but for computer scientists, knowing the powers of two is!

> *As an exercise, modify this program so that it outputs the powers of two up to 65,536 (that's 2^{16}). Print it out and memorize it.*

The backslash character in `'\t'` indicates the beginning of an **escape sequence**. Escape sequences are used to represent invisible characters like tabs and newlines. The sequence `\n` represents a newline.

An escape sequence can appear anywhere in a string; in the example, the tab escape sequence is the only thing in the string.

How do you think you represent a backslash in a string?

> *As an exercise, write a single string that*

```
produces
        this
                output.
```

6.4 Two-dimensional tables

A two-dimensional table is a table where you read the value at the intersection of a row and a column. A multiplication table is a good example. Let's say you want to print a multiplication table for the values from 1 to 6.

A good way to start is to write a loop that prints the multiples of 2, all on one line:

```
i = 1
while i <= 6:
  print 2*i, '  ',
  i = i + 1
print
```

The first line initializes a variable named `i`, which acts as a counter or **loop variable**. As the loop executes, the value of `i` increases from 1 to 6. When `i` is 7, the loop terminates. Each time through the loop, it displays the value of `2*i`, followed by three spaces.

Again, the comma in the `print` statement suppresses the newline. After the loop completes, the second `print` statement starts a new line.

The output of the program is:

```
2     4     6     8     10    12
```

So far, so good. The next step is to **encapsulate** and **generalize**.

6.5 Encapsulation and generalization

Encapsulation is the process of wrapping a piece of code in a function, allowing you to take advantage of all the things functions are good for. You have seen two examples of encapsulation: `printParity` in Section 4.5; and `isDivisible` in Section 5.4.

Generalization means taking something specific, such as printing the multiples of 2, and making it more general, such as printing the multiples of any integer.

This function encapsulates the previous loop and generalizes it to print multiples of `n`:

```
def printMultiples(n):
  i = 1
  while i <= 6:
    print n*i, '\t',
    i = i + 1
  print
```

To encapsulate, all we had to do was add the first line, which declares the name of the function and the parameter list. To generalize, all we had to do was replace the value 2 with the parameter `n`.

If we call this function with the argument 2, we get the same output as before. With the argument 3, the output is:

```
3     6     9     12    15    18
```

With the argument 4, the output is:

```
4     8     12    16    20    24
```

By now you can probably guess how to print a multiplication table—by calling `printMultiples` repeatedly with different arguments. In fact, we can use another loop:

```
i = 1
while i <= 6:
  printMultiples(i)
  i = i + 1
```

Notice how similar this loop is to the one inside `printMultiples`. All we did was replace the `print` statement with a function call.

The output of this program is a multiplication table:

```
1    2    3    4    5    6
2    4    6    8    10   12
3    6    9    12   15   18
4    8    12   16   20   24
5    10   15   20   25   30
6    12   18   24   30   36
```

6.6 More encapsulation

To demonstrate encapsulation again, let's take the code from the end of Section 6.5 and wrap it up in a function:

```
def printMultTable():
  i = 1
  while i <= 6:
    printMultiples(i)
    i = i + 1
```

This process is a common **development plan**. We develop code by writing lines of code outside any function, or typing them in to the interpreter. When we get the code working, we extract it and wrap it up in a function.

This development plan is particularly useful if you don't know, when you start writing, how to divide the program into functions. This approach lets you design as you go along.

6.7 Local variables

You might be wondering how we can use the same variable, `i`, in both `printMultiples` and `printMultTable`. Doesn't it cause problems when one of the functions changes the value of the variable?

The answer is no, because the `i` in `printMultiples` and the `i` in `printMultTable` are *not* the same variable.

Variables created inside a function definition are local; you can't access a local variable from outside its "home" function. That means you are free to have multiple variables with the same name as long as they are not in the same function.

The stack diagram for this program shows that the two variables named `i` are not the same variable. They can refer to different values, and changing one does not affect the other.

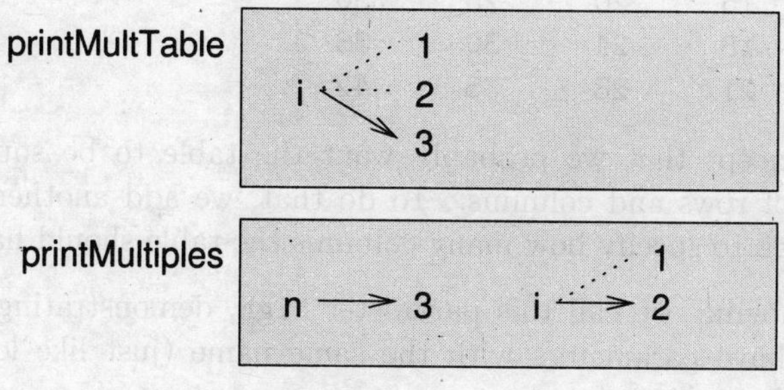

The value of `i` in `printMultTable` goes from 1 to 6. In the diagram it happens to be 3. The next time through the loop it will be 4. Each time through the loop, `printMultTable` calls `printMultiples` with the current value of `i` as an argument. That value gets assigned to the parameter `n`.

Inside `printMultiples`, the value of `i` goes from 1 to 6. In the diagram, it happens to be 2. Changing this variable has no effect on the value of `i` in `printMultTable`.

It is common and perfectly legal to have different local variables with the same name. In particular, names like `i` and `j` are used frequently as loop variables. If you avoid using them in one function just because you used them somewhere else, you will probably make the program harder to read.

6.8 More generalization

As another example of generalization, imagine you wanted a program that would print a multiplication table of any size, not just the six-by-six table. You could add a parameter to printMultTable:

```
def printMultTable(high):
  i = 1
  while i <= high:
    printMultiples(i)
    i = i + 1
```

We replaced the value 6 with the parameter high. If we call printMultTable with the argument 7, it displays:

```
1       2       3       4       5       6
2       4       6       8       10      12
3       6       9       12      15      18
4       8       12      16      20      24
5       10      15      20      25      30
6       12      18      24      30      36
7       14      21      28      35      42
```

This is fine, except that we probably want the table to be square—with the same number of rows and columns. To do that, we add another parameter to printMultiples to specify how many columns the table should have.

Just to be annoying, we call this parameter high, demonstrating that different functions can have parameters with the same name (just like local variables). Here's the whole program:

```
def printMultiples(n, high):
  i = 1
  while i <= high:
    print n*i, '\t',
    i = i + 1
  print

def printMultTable(high):
  i = 1
  while i <= high:
    printMultiples(i, high)
    i = i + 1
```

Notice that when we added a new parameter, we had to change the first line of the function (the function heading), and we also had to change the place where the function is called in `printMultTable`.

As expected, this program generates a square seven-by-seven table:

```
1       2       3       4       5       6       7
2       4       6       8       10      12      14
3       6       9       12      15      18      21
4       8       12      16      20      24      28
5       10      15      20      25      30      35
6       12      18      24      30      36      42
7       14      21      28      35      42      49
```

When you generalize a function appropriately, you often get a program with capabilities you didn't plan. For example, you might notice that, because $ab = ba$, all the entries in the table appear twice. You could save ink by printing only half the table. To do that, you only have to change one line of `printMultTable`. Change

```
    printMultiples(i, high)
```

to

```
    printMultiples(i, i)
```

and you get

```
1
2       4
3       6       9
4       8       12      16
5       10      15      20      25
6       12      18      24      30      36
7       14      21      28      35      42      49
```

As an exercise, trace the execution of this version of `printMultTable` *and figure out how it works.*

6.9 Functions

A few times now, we have mentioned "all the things functions are good for." By now, you might be wondering what exactly those things are. Here are some of them:

- Giving a name to a sequence of statements makes your program easier to read and debug.

- Dividing a long program into functions allows you to separate parts of the program, debug them in isolation, and then compose them into a whole.
- Functions facilitate both recursion and iteration.
- Well-designed functions are often useful for many programs. Once you write and debug one, you can reuse it.

6.10 Glossary

multiple assignment: Making more than one assignment to the same variable during the execution of a program.

iteration: Repeated execution of a set of statements using either a recursive function call or a loop.

loop: A statement or group of statements that execute repeatedly until a terminating condition is satisfied.

infinite loop: A loop in which the terminating condition is never satisfied.

body: The statements inside a loop.

loop variable: A variable used as part of the terminating condition of a loop.

tab: A special character that causes the cursor to move to the next tab stop on the current line.

newline: A special character that causes the cursor to move to the beginning of the next line.

cursor: An invisible marker that keeps track of where the next character will be printed.

escape sequence: An escape character (\) followed by one or more printable characters used to designate a nonprintable character.

encapsulate: To divide a large complex program into components (like functions) and isolate the components from each other (by using local variables, for example).

generalize: To replace something unnecessarily specific (like a constant value) with something appropriately general (like a variable or parameter). Generalization makes code more versatile, more likely to be reused, and sometimes even easier to write.

development plan: A process for developing a program. In this chapter, we demonstrated a style of development based on developing code to do simple, specific things and then encapsulating and generalizing.

Chapter 7

Strings

7.1 A compound data type

So far we have seen three types: `int`, `float`, and `string`. Strings are qualitatively different from the other two because they are made up of smaller pieces—characters.

Types that comprise smaller pieces are called **compound data types**. Depending on what we are doing, we may want to treat a compound data type as a single thing, or we may want to access its parts. This ambiguity is useful.

The bracket operator selects a single character from a string.

```
>>> fruit = "banana"
>>> letter = fruit[1]
>>> print letter
```

The expression `fruit[1]` selects character number 1 from `fruit`. The variable `letter` refers to the result. When we display `letter`, we get a surprise:

```
a
```

The first letter of `"banana"` is not `a`. Unless you are a computer scientist. In that case you should think of the expression in brackets as an offset from the beginning of the string, and the offset of the first letter is zero. So `b` is the 0th letter ("zero-eth") of `"banana"`, `a` is the 1th letter ("one-eth"), and `n` is the 2th ("two-eth") letter.

To get the first letter of a string, you just put 0, or any expression with the value 0, in the brackets:

```
>>> letter = fruit[0]
>>> print letter
b
```

The expression in brackets is called an **index**. An index specifies a member of an ordered set, in this case the set of characters in the string. The index *indicates* which one you want, hence the name. It can be any integer expression.

7.2 Length

The `len` function returns the number of characters in a string:

```
>>> fruit = "banana"
>>> len(fruit)
6
```

To get the last letter of a string, you might be tempted to try something like this:

```
length = len(fruit)
last = fruit[length]       # ERROR!
```

That won't work. It causes the runtime error `IndexError: string index out of range`. The reason is that there is no 6th letter in `"banana"`. Since we started counting at zero, the six letters are numbered 0 to 5. To get the last character, we have to subtract 1 from `length`:

```
length = len(fruit)
last = fruit[length-1]
```

Alternatively, we can use negative indices, which count backward from the end of the string. The expression `fruit[-1]` yields the last letter, `fruit[-2]` yields the second to last, and so on.

7.3 Traversal and the for loop

A lot of computations involve processing a string one character at a time. Often they start at the beginning, select each character in turn, do something to it, and continue until the end. This pattern of processing is called a **traversal**. One way to encode a traversal is with a `while` statement:

```
index = 0
while index < len(fruit):
  letter = fruit[index]
  print letter
  index = index + 1
```

This loop traverses the string and displays each letter on a line by itself. The loop condition is `index < len(fruit)`, so when `index` is equal to the length of the string, the condition is false, and the body of the loop is not executed. The last character accessed is the one with the index `len(fruit)-1`, which is the last character in the string.

> *As an exercise, write a function that takes a string as an argument and outputs the letters backward, one per line.*

Using an index to traverse a set of values is so common that Python provides an alternative, simpler syntax—the `for` loop:

```
for char in fruit:
  print char
```

Each time through the loop, the next character in the string is assigned to the variable `char`. The loop continues until no characters are left.

The following example shows how to use concatenation and a `for` loop to generate an abecedarian series. "Abecedarian" refers to a series or list in which the elements appear in alphabetical order. For example, in Robert McCloskey's book *Make Way for Ducklings*, the names of the ducklings are Jack, Kack, Lack, Mack, Nack, Ouack, Pack, and Quack. This loop outputs these names in order:

```
prefixes = "JKLMNOPQ"
suffix = "ack"

for letter in prefixes:
  print letter + suffix
```

The output of this program is:

```
Jack
Kack
Lack
Mack
Nack
Oack
Pack
Qack
```

Of course, that's not quite right because "Ouack" and "Quack" are misspelled.

> *As an exercise, modify the program to fix this error.*

7.4 String slices

A segment of a string is called a **slice**. Selecting a slice is similar to selecting a character:

```
>>> s = "Peter, Paul, and Mary"
>>> print s[0:5]
Peter
>>> print s[7:11]
Paul
>>> print s[17:21]
Mary
```

The operator `[n:m]` returns the part of the string from the "n-eth" character to the "m-eth" character, including the first but excluding the last. This behavior is counterintuitive; it makes more sense if you imagine the indices pointing *between* the characters, as in the following diagram:

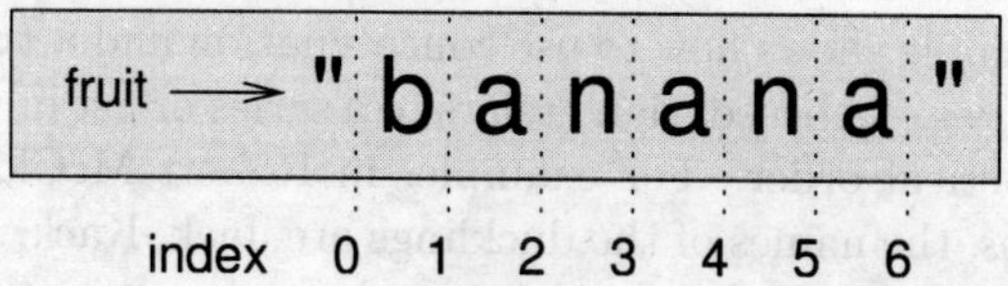

If you omit the first index (before the colon), the slice starts at the beginning of the string. If you omit the second index, the slice goes to the end of the string. Thus:

```
>>> fruit = "banana"
>>> fruit[:3]
'ban'
>>> fruit[3:]
'ana'
```

What do you think `s[:]` means?

7.5 String comparison

The comparison operators work on strings. To see if two strings are equal:

```
if word == "banana":
  print  "Yes, we have no bananas!"
```

Other comparison operations are useful for putting words in alphabetical order:

```
if word < "banana":
  print "Your word," + word + ", comes before banana."
elif word > "banana":
  print "Your word," + word + ", comes after banana."
else:
  print "Yes, we have no bananas!"
```

You should be aware, though, that Python does not handle upper- and lowercase letters the same way that people do. All the uppercase letters come before all the lowercase letters. As a result:

```
Your word, Zebra, comes before banana.
```

A common way to address this problem is to convert strings to a standard format, such as all lowercase, before performing the comparison. A more difficult problem is making the program realize that zebras are not fruit.

7.6 Strings are immutable

It is tempting to use the `[]` operator on the left side of an assignment, with the intention of changing a character in a string. For example:

```
greeting = "Hello, world!"
greeting[0] = 'J'            # ERROR!
print greeting
```

Instead of producing the output `Jello, world!`, this code produces the runtime error `TypeError: object doesn't support item assignment`.

Strings are **immutable**, which means you can't change an existing string. The best you can do is create a new string that is a variation on the original:

```
greeting = "Hello, world!"
newGreeting = 'J' + greeting[1:]
print newGreeting
```

The solution here is to concatenate a new first letter onto a slice of `greeting`. This operation has no effect on the original string.

7.7 A `find` function

What does the following function do?

```
def find(str, ch):
  index = 0
  while index < len(str):
    if str[index] == ch:
      return index
    index = index + 1
  return -1
```

In a sense, `find` is the opposite of the `[]` operator. Instead of taking an index and extracting the corresponding character, it takes a character and finds the index where that character appears. If the character is not found, the function returns `-1`.

This is the first example we have seen of a `return` statement inside a loop. If `str[index] == ch`, the function returns immediately, breaking out of the loop prematurely.

If the character doesn't appear in the string, then the program exits the loop normally and returns `-1`.

This pattern of computation is sometimes called a "eureka" traversal because as soon as we find what we are looking for, we can cry "Eureka!" and stop looking.

> *As an exercise, modify the* `find` *function so that it has a third parameter, the index in the string where it should start looking.*

7.8 Looping and counting

The following program counts the number of times the letter `a` appears in a string:

```
fruit = "banana"
count = 0
for char in fruit:
  if char == 'a':
    count = count + 1
print count
```

This program demonstrates another pattern of computation called a **counter**. The variable `count` is initialized to 0 and then incremented each time an `a` is found. (To **increment** is to increase by one; it is the opposite of **decrement**, and unrelated to "excrement," which is a noun.) When the loop exits, `count` contains the result—the total number of `a`'s.

As an exercise, encapsulate this code in a function named `countLetters`, *and generalize it so that it accepts the string and the letter as arguments.*

As a second exercise, rewrite this function so that instead of traversing the string, it uses the three-parameter version of `find` *from the previous.*

7.9 The string module

The `string` module contains useful functions that manipulate strings. As usual, we have to import the module before we can use it:

```
>>> import string
```

The `string` module includes a function named `find` that does the same thing as the function we wrote. To call it we have to specify the name of the module and the name of the function using dot notation.

```
>>> fruit = "banana"
>>> index = string.find(fruit, "a")
>>> print index
1
```

This example demonstrates one of the benefits of modules—they help avoid collisions between the names of built-in functions and user-defined functions. By using dot notation we can specify which version of `find` we want.

Actually, `string.find` is more general than our version. First, it can find substrings, not just characters:

```
>>> string.find("banana", "na")
2
```

Also, it takes an additional argument that specifies the index it should start at:

```
>>> string.find("banana", "na", 3)
4
```

Or it can take two additional arguments that specify a range of indices:

```
>>> string.find("bob", "b", 1, 2)
-1
```

In this example, the search fails because the letter *b* does not appear in the index range from `1` to `2` (not including `2`).

7.10 Character classification

It is often helpful to examine a character and test whether it is upper- or lowercase, or whether it is a character or a digit. The `string` module provides several constants that are useful for these purposes.

The string `string.lowercase` contains all of the letters that the system considers to be lowercase. Similarly, `string.uppercase` contains all of the uppercase letters. Try the following and see what you get:

```
>>> print string.lowercase
>>> print string.uppercase
>>> print string.digits
```

We can use these constants and `find` to classify characters. For example, if `find(lowercase, ch)` returns a value other than `-1`, then `ch` must be lowercase:

```
def isLower(ch):
  return string.find(string.lowercase, ch) != -1
```

Alternatively, we can take advantage of the `in` operator, which determines whether a character appears in a string:

```
def isLower(ch):
  return ch in string.lowercase
```

As yet another alternative, we can use the comparison operator:

```
def isLower(ch):
  return 'a' <= ch <= 'z'
```

If `ch` is between *a* and *z*, it must be a lowercase letter.

> *As an exercise, discuss which version of* `isLower` *you think will be fastest. Can you think of other reasons besides speed to prefer one or the other?*

Another constant defined in the `string` module may surprise you when you print it:

```
>>> print string.whitespace
```

Whitespace characters move the cursor without printing anything. They create the white space between visible characters (at least on white paper). The constant `string.whitespace` contains all the whitespace characters, including space, tab (`\t`), and newline (`\n`).

There are other useful functions in the `string` module, but this book isn't intended to be a reference manual. On the other hand, the *Python Library Reference* is. Along with a wealth of other documentation, it's available from the Python website, `www.python.org`.

7.11 Glossary

compound data type: A data type in which the values are made up of components, or elements, that are themselves values.

traverse: To iterate through the elements of a set, performing a similar operation on each.

index: A variable or value used to select a member of an ordered set, such as a character from a string.

slice: A part of a string specified by a range of indices.

mutable: A compound data types whose elements can be assigned new values.

counter: A variable used to count something, usually initialized to zero and then incremented.

increment: To increase the value of a variable by one.

decrement: To decrease the value of a variable by one.

whitespace: Any of the characters that move the cursor without printing visible characters. The constant `string.whitespace` contains all the whitespace characters.

Chapter 8

Lists

A **list** is an ordered set of values, where each value is identified by an index. The values that make up a list are called its **elements**. Lists are similar to strings, which are ordered sets of characters, except that the elements of a list can have any type. Lists and strings—and other things that behave like ordered sets—are called **sequences**.

8.1 List values

There are several ways to create a new list; the simplest is to enclose the elements in square brackets ([and]):

```
[10, 20, 30, 40]
["spam", "bungee", "swallow"]
```

The first example is a list of four integers. The second is a list of three strings. The elements of a list don't have to be the same type. The following list contains a string, a float, an integer, and (mirabile dictu) another list:

```
["hello", 2.0, 5, [10, 20]]
```

A list within another list is said to be **nested**.

Lists that contain consecutive integers are common, so Python provides a simple way to create them:

```
>>> range(1,5)
[1, 2, 3, 4]
```

The range function takes two arguments and returns a list that contains all the integers from the first to the second, including the first but not including the second!

There are two other forms of range. With a single argument, it creates a list that starts at 0:

```
>>> range(10)
[0, 1, 2, 3, 4, 5, 6, 7, 8, 9]
```

If there is a third argument, it specifies the space between successive values, which is called the **step size**. This example counts from 1 to 10 by steps of 2:

```
>>> range(1, 10, 2)
[1, 3, 5, 7, 9]
```

Finally, there is a special list that contains no elements. It is called the empty list, and it is denoted [].

With all these ways to create lists, it would be disappointing if we couldn't assign list values to variables or pass lists as arguments to functions. We can.

```
vocabulary = ["ameliorate", "castigate", "defenestrate"]
numbers = [17, 123]
empty = []
print vocabulary, numbers, empty
['ameliorate', 'castigate', 'defenestrate'] [17, 123] []
```

8.2 Accessing elements

The syntax for accessing the elements of a list is the same as the syntax for accessing the characters of a string—the bracket operator ([]). The expression inside the brackets specifies the index. Remember that the indices start at 0:

```
print numbers[0]
numbers[1] = 5
```

The bracket operator can appear anywhere in an expression. When it appears on the left side of an assignment, it changes one of the elements in the list, so the one-eth element of numbers, which used to be 123, is now 5.

Any integer expression can be used as an index:

```
>>> numbers[3-2]
5
>>> numbers[1.0]
TypeError: sequence index must be integer
```

If you try to read or write an element that does not exist, you get a runtime error:

```
>>> numbers[2] = 5
IndexError: list assignment index out of range
```

If an index has a negative value, it counts backward from the end of the list:

```
>>> numbers[-1]
5
>>> numbers[-2]
17
>>> numbers[-3]
IndexError: list index out of range
```

`numbers[-1]` is the last element of the list, `numbers[-2]` is the second to last, and `numbers[-3]` doesn't exist.

It is common to use a loop variable as a list index.

```
horsemen = ["war", "famine", "pestilence", "death"]

i = 0
while i < 4:
  print horsemen[i]
  i = i + 1
```

This `while` loop counts from 0 to 4. When the loop variable `i` is 4, the condition fails and the loop terminates. So the body of the loop is only executed when `i` is 0, 1, 2, and 3.

Each time through the loop, the variable `i` is used as an index into the list, printing the `i`-eth element. This pattern of computation is called a **list traversal**.

8.3 List length

The function `len` returns the length of a list. It is a good idea to use this value as the upper bound of a loop instead of a constant. That way, if the size of the list changes, you won't have to go through the program changing all the loops; they will work correctly for any size list:

```
horsemen = ["war", "famine", "pestilence", "death"]

i = 0
while i < len(horsemen):
  print horsemen[i]
  i = i + 1
```

The last time the body of the loop is executed, `i` is `len(horsemen) - 1`, which is the index of the last element. When `i` is equal to `len(horsemen)`, the condition fails and the body is not executed, which is a good thing, because `len(horsemen)` is not a legal index.

Although a list can contain another list, the nested list still counts as a single element. The length of this list is four:

```
['spam!', 1, ['Brie', 'Roquefort', 'Pol le Veq'], [1, 2, 3]]
```

> *As an exercise, write a loop that traverses the previous list and prints the length of each element. What happens if you send an integer to* `len`*?*

8.4 List membership

`in` is a boolean operator that tests membership in a sequence. We used it in Section 7.10 with strings, but it also works with lists and other sequences:

```
>>> horsemen = ['war', 'famine', 'pestilence', 'death']
>>> 'pestilence' in horsemen
True
>>> 'debauchery' in horsemen
False
```

Since "pestilence" is a member of the `horsemen` list, the `in` operator returns true. Since "debauchery" is not in the list, `in` returns false.

We can use the `not` in combination with `in` to test whether an element is not a member of a list:

```
>>> 'debauchery' not in horsemen
True
```

8.5 Lists and for loops

The `for` loop we saw in Section 7.3 also works with lists. The generalized syntax of a `for` loop is:

```
for VARIABLE in LIST:
  BODY
```

This statement is equivalent to:

```
i = 0
while i < len(LIST):
  VARIABLE = LIST[i]
  BODY
  i = i + 1
```

The `for` loop is more concise because we can eliminate the loop variable, `i`. Here is the previous loop written with a `for` loop.

```
for horseman in horsemen:
  print horseman
```

It almost reads like English: "For (every) horseman in (the list of) horsemen, print (the name of the) horseman."

Any list expression can be used in a `for` loop:

```
for number in range(20):
  if number % 2 == 0:
    print  number

for fruit in ["banana", "apple", "quince"]:
  print "I like to eat " + fruit + "s!"
```

The first example prints all the even numbers between zero and nineteen. The second example expresses enthusiasm for various fruits.

8.6 List operations

The `+` operator concatenates lists:

```
>>> a = [1, 2, 3]
>>> b = [4, 5, 6]
>>> c = a + b
>>> print c
[1, 2, 3, 4, 5, 6]
```

Similarly, the `*` operator repeats a list a given number of times:

```
>>> [0] * 4
[0, 0, 0, 0]
>>> [1, 2, 3] * 3
[1, 2, 3, 1, 2, 3, 1, 2, 3]
```

The first example repeats `[0]` four times. The second example repeats the list `[1, 2, 3]` three times.

8.7 List slices

The slice operations we saw in Section 7.4 also work on lists:

```
>>> list = ['a', 'b', 'c', 'd', 'e', 'f']
>>> list[1:3]
['b', 'c']
>>> list[:4]
['a', 'b', 'c', 'd']
>>> list[3:]
['d', 'e', 'f']
```

If you omit the first index, the slice starts at the beginning. If you omit the second, the slice goes to the end. So if you omit both, the slice is really a copy of the whole list.

```
>>> list[:]
['a', 'b', 'c', 'd', 'e', 'f']
```

8.8 Lists are mutable

Unlike strings, lists are mutable, which means we can change their elements. Using the bracket operator on the left side of an assignment, we can update one of the elements:

```
>>> fruit = ["banana", "apple", "quince"]
>>> fruit[0] = "pear"
>>> fruit[-1] = "orange"
>>> print fruit
['pear', 'apple', 'orange']
```

With the slice operator we can update several elements at once:

```
>>> list = ['a', 'b', 'c', 'd', 'e', 'f']
>>> list[1:3] = ['x', 'y']
>>> print list
['a', 'x', 'y', 'd', 'e', 'f']
```

We can also remove elements from a list by assigning the empty list to them:

```
>>> list = ['a', 'b', 'c', 'd', 'e', 'f']
>>> list[1:3] = []
>>> print list
['a', 'd', 'e', 'f']
```

And we can add elements to a list by squeezing them into an empty slice at the desired location:

```
>>> list = ['a', 'd', 'f']
>>> list[1:1] = ['b', 'c']
>>> print list
['a', 'b', 'c', 'd', 'f']
>>> list[4:4] = ['e']
>>> print list
['a', 'b', 'c', 'd', 'e', 'f']
```

8.9 List deletion

Using slices to delete list elements can be awkward, and therefore error-prone. Python provides an alternative that is more readable.

`del` removes an element from a list:

```
>>> a = ['one', 'two', 'three']
>>> del a[1]
>>> a
['one', 'three']
```

As you might expect, `del` handles negative indices and causes a runtime error if the index is out of range.

You can use a slice as an index for `del`:

```
>>> list = ['a', 'b', 'c', 'd', 'e', 'f']
>>> del list[1:5]
>>> print list
['a', 'f']
```

As usual, slices select all the elements up to, but not including, the second index.

8.10 Objects and values

If we execute these assignment statements,

```
a = "banana"
b = "banana"
```

we know that `a` and `b` will refer to a string with the letters `"banana"`. But we can't tell whether they point to the *same* string.

There are two possible states:

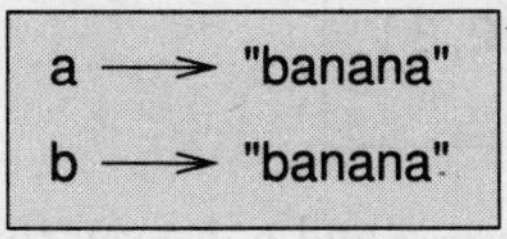

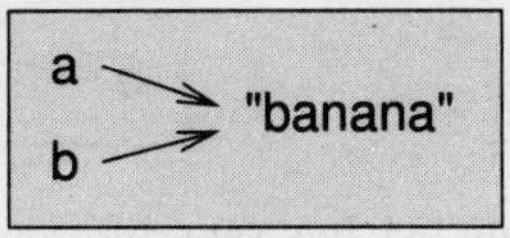

In one case, `a` and `b` refer to two different things that have the same value. In the second case, they refer to the same thing. These "things" have names—they are called **objects**. An object is something a variable can refer to.

Every object has a unique **identifier**, which we can obtain with the `id` function. By printing the identifier of `a` and `b`, we can tell whether they refer to the same object.

```
>>> id(a)
135044008
>>> id(b)
135044008
```

In fact, we get the same identifier twice, which means that Python only created one string, and both `a` and `b` refer to it.

Interestingly, lists behave differently. When we create two lists, we get two objects:

```
>>> a = [1, 2, 3]
>>> b = [1, 2, 3]
>>> id(a)
135045528
>>> id(b)
135041704
```

So the state diagram looks like this:

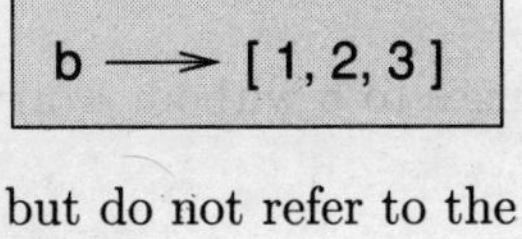

`a` and `b` have the same value but do not refer to the same object.

8.11 Aliasing

Since variables refer to objects, if we assign one variable to another, both variables refer to the same object:

```
>>> a = [1, 2, 3]
>>> b = a
```

In this case, the state diagram looks like this:

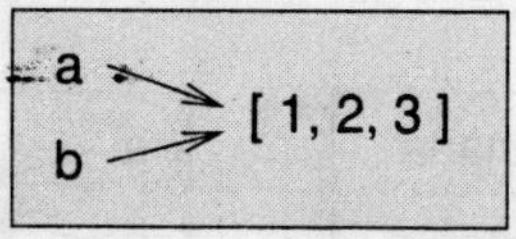

Because the same list has two different names, a and b, we say that it is **aliased**. Changes made with one alias affect the other:

```
>>> b[0] = 5
>>> print a
[5, 2, 3]
```

Although this behavior can be useful, it is sometimes unexpected or undesirable. In general, it is safer to avoid aliasing when you are working with mutable objects. Of course, for immutable objects, there's no problem. That's why Python is free to alias strings when it sees an opportunity to economize.

8.12 Cloning lists

If we want to modify a list and also keep a copy of the original, we need to be able to make a copy of the list itself, not just the reference. This process is sometimes called **cloning**, to avoid the ambiguity of the word "copy."

The easiest way to clone a list is to use the slice operator:

```
>>> a = [1, 2, 3]
>>> b = a[:]
>>> print b
[1, 2, 3]
```

Taking any slice of a creates a new list. In this case the slice happens to consist of the whole list.

Now we are free to make changes to b without worrying about a:

```
>>> b[0] = 5
>>> print a
[1, 2, 3]
```

As an exercise, draw a state diagram for `a` *and* `b` *before and after this change.*

8.13 List parameters

Passing a list as an argument actually passes a reference to the list, not a copy of the list. For example, the function **head** takes a list as an argument and returns the first element:

```
def head(list):
  return list[0]
```

Here's how it is used:

```
>>> numbers = [1, 2, 3]
>>> head(numbers)
1
```

The parameter `list` and the variable `numbers` are aliases for the same object. The state diagram looks like this:

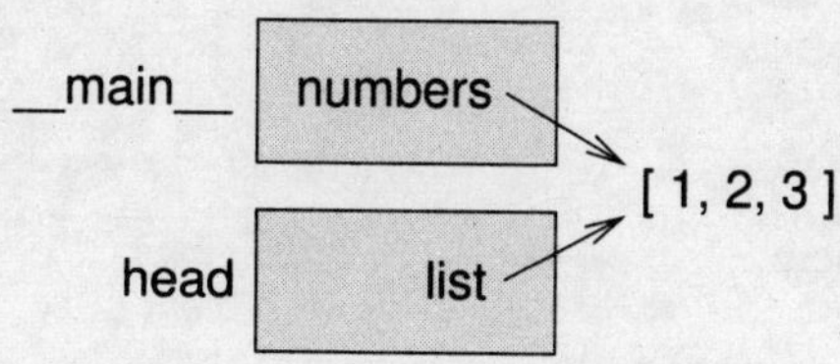

Since the list object is shared by two frames, we drew it between them.

If a function modifies a list parameter, the caller sees the change. For example, `deleteHead` removes the first element from a list:

```
def deleteHead(list):
  del list[0]
```

Here's how `deleteHead` is used:

```
>>> numbers = [1, 2, 3]
>>> deleteHead(numbers)
>>> print numbers
[2, 3]
```

If a function returns a list, it returns a reference to the list. For example, `tail` returns a list that contains all but the first element of the given list:

```
def tail(list):
  return list[1:]
```

Here's how `tail` is used:

```
>>> numbers = [1, 2, 3]
>>> rest = tail(numbers)
>>> print rest
[2, 3]
```

Because the return value was created with the slice operator, it is a new list. Creating `rest`, and any subsequent changes to `rest`, have no effect on `numbers`.

8.14 Nested lists

A nested list is a list that appears as an element in another list. In this list, the three-eth element is a nested list:

```
>>> list = ["hello", 2.0, 5, [10, 20]]
```

If we print `list[3]`, we get `[10, 20]`. To extract an element from the nested list, we can proceed in two steps:

```
>>> elt = list[3]
>>> elt[0]
10
```

Or we can combine them:

```
>>> list[3][1]
20
```

Bracket operators evaluate from left to right, so this expression gets the three-eth element of `list` and extracts the one-eth element from it.

8.15 Matrices

Nested lists are often used to represent matrices. For example, the matrix:

$$\begin{bmatrix} 1 & 2 & 3 \\ 4 & 5 & 6 \\ 7 & 8 & 9 \end{bmatrix}$$

might be represented as:

```
>>> matrix = [[1, 2, 3], [4, 5, 6], [7, 8, 9]]
```

`matrix` is a list with three elements, where each element is a row of the matrix. We can select an entire row from the matrix in the usual way:

```
>>> matrix[1]
[4, 5, 6]
```

Or we can extract a single element from the matrix using the double-index form:

```
>>> matrix[1][1]
5
```

The first index selects the row, and the second index selects the column. Although this way of representing matrices is common, it is not the only possibility. A small variation is to use a list of columns instead of a list of rows. Later we will see a more radical alternative using a dictionary.

8.16 Strings and lists

Two of the most useful functions in the `string` module involve lists of strings. The `split` function breaks a string into a list of words. By default, any number of whitespace characters is considered a word boundary:

```
>>> import string
>>> song = "The rain in Spain..."
>>> string.split(song)
['The', 'rain', 'in', 'Spain...']
```

An optional argument called a **delimiter** can be used to specify which characters to use as word boundaries. The following example uses the string `ai` as the delimiter:

```
>>> string.split(song, 'ai')
['The r', 'n in Sp', 'n...']
```

Notice that the delimiter doesn't appear in the list.

The `join` function is the inverse of `split`. It takes a list of strings and concatenates the elements with a space between each pair:

```
>>> list = ['The', 'rain', 'in', 'Spain...']
>>> string.join(list)
'The rain in Spain...'
```

Like split, join takes an optional delimiter that is inserted between elements:

```
>>> string.join(list, '_')
'The_rain_in_Spain...'
```

> *As an exercise, describe the relationship between* `string.join(string.split(song))` *and* `song`*. Are they the same for all strings? When would they be different?*

8.17 Glossary

list: A named collection of objects, where each object is identified by an index.

index: An integer variable or value that indicates an element of a list.

element: One of the values in a list (or other sequence). The bracket operator selects elements of a list.

sequence: Any of the data types that consist of an ordered set of elements, with each element identified by an index.

nested list: A list that is an element of another list.

list traversal: The sequential accessing of each element in a list.

object: A thing to which a variable can refer.

aliases: Multiple variables that contain references to the same object.

clone: To create a new object that has the same value as an existing object. Copying a reference to an object creates an alias but doesn't clone the object.

delimiter: A character or string used to indicate where a string should be split.

Chapter 9

Tuples

9.1 Mutability and tuples

So far, you have seen two compound types: strings, which are made up of characters; and lists, which are made up of elements of any type. One of the differences we noted is that the elements of a list can be modified, but the characters in a string cannot. In other words, strings are **immutable** and lists are **mutable**.

There is another type in Python called a **tuple** that is similar to a list except that it is immutable. Syntactically, a tuple is a comma-separated list of values:

```
>>> tuple = 'a', 'b', 'c', 'd', 'e'
```

Although it is not necessary, it is conventional to enclose tuples in parentheses:

```
>>> tuple = ('a', 'b', 'c', 'd', 'e')
```

To create a tuple with a single element, we have to include the final comma:

```
>>> t1 = ('a',)
>>> type(t1)
<type 'tuple'>
```

Without the comma, Python treats ('a') as a string in parentheses:

```
>>> t2 = ('a')
>>> type(t2)
<type 'str'>
```

Syntax issues aside, the operations on tuples are the same as the operations on lists. The index operator selects an element from a tuple.

```
>>> tuple = ('a', 'b', 'c', 'd', 'e')
>>> tuple[0]
'a'
```

And the slice operator selects a range of elements.

```
>>> tuple[1:3]
('b', 'c')
```

But if we try to modify one of the elements of the tuple, we get an error:

```
>>> tuple[0] = 'A'
TypeError: object doesn't support item assignment
```

Of course, even if we can't modify the elements of a tuple, we can replace it with a different tuple:

```
>>> tuple = ('A',) + tuple[1:]
>>> tuple
('A', 'b', 'c', 'd', 'e')
```

9.2 Tuple assignment

Once in a while, it is useful to swap the values of two variables. With conventional assignment statements, we have to use a temporary variable. For example, to swap a and b:

```
>>> temp = a
>>> a = b
>>> b = temp
```

If we have to do this often, this approach becomes cumbersome. Python provides a form of **tuple assignment** that solves this problem neatly:

```
>>> a, b = b, a
```

The left side is a tuple of variables; the right side is a tuple of values. Each value is assigned to its respective variable. All the expressions on the right side are evaluated before any of the assignments. This feature makes tuple assignment quite versatile.

Naturally, the number of variables on the left and the number of values on the right have to be the same:

```
>>> a, b, c, d = 1, 2, 3
ValueError: unpack tuple of wrong size
```

9.3 Tuples as return values

Functions can return tuples as return values. For example, we could write a function that swaps two parameters:

```
def swap(x, y):
  return y, x
```

Then we can assign the return value to a tuple with two variables:

```
a, b = swap(a, b)
```

In this case, there is no great advantage in making `swap` a function. In fact, there is a danger in trying to encapsulate `swap`, which is the following tempting mistake:

```
def swap(x, y):          # incorrect version
  x, y = y, x
```

If we call this function like this:

```
swap(a, b)
```

then `a` and `x` are aliases for the same value. Changing `x` inside `swap` makes `x` refer to a different value, but it has no effect on `a` in `__main__`. Similarly, changing `y` has no effect on `b`.

This function runs without producing an error message, but it doesn't do what we intended. This is an example of a semantic error.

> *As an exercise, draw a state diagram for this function so that you can see why it doesn't work.*

9.4 Random numbers

Most computer programs do the same thing every time they execute, so they are said to be **deterministic**. Determinism is usually a good thing, since we expect the same calculation to yield the same result. For some applications, though, we want the computer to be unpredictable. Games are an obvious example, but there are more.

Making a program truly nondeterministic turns out to be not so easy, but there are ways to make it at least seem nondeterministic. One of them is to generate random numbers and use them to determine the outcome of the program. Python provides a built-in function that generates **pseudorandom** numbers, which are not truly random in the mathematical sense, but for our purposes they will do.

The `random` module contains a function called `random` that returns a floating-point number between 0.0 and 1.0. Each time you call `random`, you get the next number in a long series. To see a sample, run this loop:

```
import random

for i in range(10):
  x = random.random()
  print x
```

To generate a random number between 0.0 and an upper bound like `high`, multiply `x` by `high`.

> *As an exercise, generate a random number between* `low` *and* `high`.

> *As an additional exercise, generate a random* integer *between* `low` *and* `high`*, including both end points.*

9.5 List of random numbers

The first step is to generate a list of random values. `randomList` takes an integer argument and returns a list of random numbers with the given length. It starts with a list of `n` zeros. Each time through the loop, it replaces one of the elements with a random number. The return value is a reference to the complete list:

```
def randomList(n):
  s = [0] * n
  for i in range(n):
    s[i] = random.random()
  return s
```

We'll test this function with a list of eight elements. For purposes of debugging, it is a good idea to start small.

```
>>> randomList(8)
0.15156642489
0.498048560109
0.810894847068
0.360371157682
0.275119183077
0.328578797631
0.759199803101
0.800367163582
```

The numbers generated by `random` are supposed to be distributed uniformly, which means that every value is equally likely.

If we divide the range of possible values into equal-sized "buckets," and count the number of times a random value falls in each bucket, we should get roughly the same number in each.

We can test this theory by writing a program to divide the range into buckets and count the number of values in each.

9.6 Counting

A good approach to problems like this is to divide the problem into subproblems and look for subproblems that fit a computational pattern you have seen before.

In this case, we want to traverse a list of numbers and count the number of times a value falls in a given range. That sounds familiar. In Section 7.8, we wrote a program that traversed a string and counted the number of times a given letter appeared.

So, we can proceed by copying the old program and adapting it for the current problem. The original program was:

```
count = 0
for char in fruit:
  if char == 'a':
    count = count + 1
print count
```

The first step is to replace `fruit` with `t` and `char` with `num`. That doesn't change the program; it just makes it more readable.

The second step is to change the test. We aren't interested in finding letters. We want to see if `num` is between the given values `low` and `high`.

```
count = 0
for num in t:
  if low < num < high:
    count = count + 1
print count
```

The last step is to encapsulate this code in a function called **inBucket**. The parameters are the list and the values `low` and `high`.

```
def inBucket(t, low, high):
  count = 0
  for num in t:
    if low < num < high:
      count = count + 1
  return count
```

By copying and modifying an existing program, we were able to write this function quickly and save a lot of debugging time. This development plan is called **pattern matching**. If you find yourself working on a problem you have solved before, reuse the solution.

9.7 Many buckets

As the number of buckets increases, `inBucket` gets a little unwieldy. With two buckets, it's not bad:

```
low = inBucket(a, 0.0, 0.5)
high = inBucket(a, 0.5, 1)
```

But with four buckets it is getting cumbersome.

```
bucket1 = inBucket(a, 0.0, 0.25)
bucket2 = inBucket(a, 0.25, 0.5)
bucket3 = inBucket(a, 0.5, 0.75)
bucket4 = inBucket(a, 0.75, 1.0)
```

There are two problems. One is that we have to make up new variable names for each result. The other is that we have to compute the range for each bucket.

We'll solve the second problem first. If the number of buckets is `numBuckets`, then the width of each bucket is `1.0 / numBuckets`.

We'll use a loop to compute the range of each bucket. The loop variable, `i`, counts from 0 to `numBuckets-1`:

```
bucketWidth = 1.0 / numBuckets
for i in range(numBuckets):
  low = i * bucketWidth
  high = low + bucketWidth
  print low, "to", high
```

To compute the low end of each bucket, we multiply the loop variable by the bucket width. The high end is just a `bucketWidth` away.

With `numBuckets = 8`, the output is:

```
0.0 to 0.125
0.125 to 0.25
0.25 to 0.375
0.375 to 0.5
0.5 to 0.625
0.625 to 0.75
0.75 to 0.875
0.875 to 1.0
```

You can confirm that each bucket is the same width, that they don't overlap, and that they cover the entire range from 0.0 to 1.0.

Now back to the first problem. We need a way to store eight integers, using the loop variable to indicate one at a time. By now you should be thinking, "List!"

We have to create the bucket list outside the loop, because we only want to do it once. Inside the loop, we'll call `inBucket` repeatedly and update the `i`-eth element of the list:

```
numBuckets = 8
buckets = [0] * numBuckets
bucketWidth = 1.0 / numBuckets
for i in range(numBuckets):
  low = i * bucketWidth
  high = low + bucketWidth
  buckets[i] = inBucket(t, low, high)
print buckets
```

With a list of 1000 values, this code produces this bucket list:

```
[138, 124, 128, 118, 130, 117, 114, 131]
```

These numbers are fairly close to 125, which is what we expected. At least, they are close enough that we can believe the random number generator is working.

> *As an exercise, test this function with some longer lists, and see if the number of values in each bucket tends to level off.*

9.8 A single-pass solution

Although this program works, it is not as efficient as it could be. Every time it calls `inBucket`, it traverses the entire list. As the number of buckets increases, that gets to be a lot of traversals.

It would be better to make a single pass through the list and compute for each value the index of the bucket in which it falls. Then we can increment the appropriate counter.

In the previous section we took an index, `i`, and multiplied it by the `bucketWidth` to find the lower bound of a given bucket. Now we want to take a value in the range 0.0 to 1.0 and find the index of the bucket where it falls.

Since this problem is the inverse of the previous problem, we might guess that we should divide by `bucketWidth` instead of multiplying. That guess is correct.

Since `bucketWidth = 1.0 / numBuckets`, dividing by `bucketWidth` is the same as multiplying by `numBuckets`. If we multiply a number in the range 0.0 to 1.0 by `numBuckets`, we get a number in the range from 0.0 to `numBuckets`. If we round that number to the next lower integer, we get exactly what we are looking for—a bucket index:

```
numBuckets = 8
buckets = [0] * numBuckets
for i in t:
  index = int(i * numBuckets)
  buckets[index] = buckets[index] + 1
```

We used the `int` function to convert a floating-point number to an integer.

Is it possible for this calculation to produce an index that is out of range (either negative or greater than `len(buckets)-1`)?

A list like `buckets` that contains counts of the number of values in each range is called a **histogram**.

> *As an exercise, write a function called* `histogram` *that takes a list and a number of buckets as arguments and returns a histogram with the given number of buckets.*

9.9 Glossary

immutable type: A type in which the elements cannot be modified. Assignments to elements or slices of immutable types cause an error.

mutable type: A data type in which the elements can be modified. All mutable types are compound types. Lists and dictionaries are mutable data types; strings and tuples are not.

tuple: A sequence type that is similar to a list except that it is immutable. Tuples can be used wherever an immutable type is required, such as a key in a dictionary.

tuple assignment: An assignment to all of the elements in a tuple using a single assignment statement. Tuple assignment occurs in parallel rather than in sequence, making it useful for swapping values.

deterministic: A program that does the same thing each time it is called.

pseudorandom: A sequence of numbers that appear to be random but that are actually the result of a deterministic computation.

histogram: A list of integers in which each element counts the number of times something happens.

pattern matching: A program development plan that involves identifying a familiar computational pattern and copying the solution to a similar problem.

9.9 Glossary

immutable type: A type in which the elements cannot be modified. Assignments to elements or slices of immutable types cause an error.

mutable type: A data type in which the elements can be modified. All mutable types are compound types. Lists and dictionaries are mutable data types; strings and tuples are not.

tuple: A sequence type that is similar to a list except that it is immutable. Tuples can be used wherever an immutable type is required, such as a key in a dictionary.

tuple assignment: An assignment to all of the elements in a tuple using a single assignment statement. Tuple assignment occurs in parallel rather than in sequence, making it useful for swapping values.

deterministic: A program that does the same thing each time it is called.

pseudorandom: A sequence of numbers that appear to be random but that are actually the result of a deterministic computation.

histogram: A list of integers in which each element counts the number of times something happens.

pattern matching: A program development plan that involves identifying a familiar computational pattern and copying the solution to a similar problem.

Chapter 10

Dictionaries

The compound types you have learned about—strings, lists, and tuples—use integers as indices. If you try to use any other type as an index, you get an error.

Dictionaries are similar to other compound types except that they can use any immutable type as an index. As an example, we will create a dictionary to translate English words into Spanish. For this dictionary, the indices are `strings`.

One way to create a dictionary is to start with the empty dictionary and add elements. The empty dictionary is denoted `{}`:

```
>>> eng2sp = {}
>>> eng2sp['one'] = 'uno'
>>> eng2sp['two'] = 'dos'
```

The first assignment creates a dictionary named `eng2sp`; the other assignments add new elements to the dictionary. We can print the current value of the dictionary in the usual way:

```
>>> print eng2sp
{'one': 'uno', 'two': 'dos'}
```

The elements of a dictionary appear in a comma-separated list. Each entry contains an index and a value separated by a colon. In a dictionary, the indices are called **keys**, so the elements are called **key-value pairs**.

Another way to create a dictionary is to provide a list of key-value pairs using the same syntax as the previous output:

```
>>> eng2sp = {'one': 'uno', 'two': 'dos', 'three': 'tres'}
```

If we print the value of eng2sp again, we get a surprise:

```
>>> print eng2sp
{'one': 'uno', 'three': 'tres', 'two': 'dos'}
```

The key-value pairs are not in order! Fortunately, there is no reason to care about the order, since the elements of a dictionary are never indexed with integer indices. Instead, we use the keys to look up the corresponding values:

```
>>> print eng2sp['two']
'dos'
```

The key 'two' yields the value 'dos' even though it appears in the third key-value pair.

10.1 Dictionary operations

The del statement removes a key-value pair from a dictionary. For example, the following dictionary contains the names of various fruits and the number of each fruit in stock:

```
>>> inventory = {'apples': 430, 'bananas': 312, 'oranges': 525,
'pears': 217}
>>> print inventory
{'oranges': 525, 'apples': 430, 'pears': 217, 'bananas': 312}
```

If someone buys all of the pears, we can remove the entry from the dictionary:

```
>>> del inventory['pears']
>>> print inventory
{'oranges': 525, 'apples': 430, 'bananas': 312}
```

Or if we're expecting more pears soon, we might just change the value associated with pears:

```
>>> inventory['pears'] = 0
>>> print inventory
{'oranges': 525, 'apples': 430, 'pears': 0, 'bananas': 312}
```

The len function also works on dictionaries; it returns the number of key-value pairs:

```
>>> len(inventory)
4
```

10.2 Dictionary methods

A **method** is similar to a function—it takes arguments and returns a value—but the syntax is different. For example, the `keys` method takes a dictionary and returns a list of the keys that appear, but instead of the function syntax `keys(eng2sp)`, we use the method syntax `eng2sp.keys()`.

```
>>> eng2sp.keys()
['one', 'three', 'two']
```

This form of dot notation specifies the name of the function, `keys`, and the name of the object to apply the function to, `eng2sp`. The parentheses indicate that this method has no parameters.

A method call is called an **invocation**; in this case, we would say that we are invoking `keys` on the object `eng2sp`.

The `values` method is similar; it returns a list of the values in the dictionary:

```
>>> eng2sp.values()
['uno', 'tres', 'dos']
```

The `items` method returns both, in the form of a list of tuples—one for each key-value pair:

```
>>> eng2sp.items()
[('one','uno'), ('three', 'tres'), ('two', 'dos')]
```

The syntax provides useful type information. The square brackets indicate that this is a list. The parentheses indicate that the elements of the list are tuples.

If a method takes an argument, it uses the same syntax as a function call. For example, the method `has_key` takes a key and returns true (1) if the key appears in the dictionary:

```
>>> eng2sp.has_key('one')
True
>>> eng2sp.has_key('deux')
False
```

If you try to call a method without specifying an object, you get an error. In this case, the error message is not very helpful:

```
>>> has_key('one')
NameError: has_key
```

10.3 Aliasing and copying

Because dictionaries are mutable, you need to be aware of aliasing. Whenever two variables refer to the same object, changes to one affect the other.

If you want to modify a dictionary and keep a copy of the original, use the copy method. For example, opposites is a dictionary that contains pairs of opposites:

```
>>> opposites = {'up': 'down', 'right': 'wrong', 'true': 'false'}
>>> alias = opposites
>>> copy = opposites.copy()
```

alias and opposites refer to the same object; copy refers to a fresh copy of the same dictionary. If we modify alias, opposites is also changed:

```
>>> alias['right'] = 'left'
>>> opposites['right']
'left'
```

If we modify copy, opposites is unchanged:

```
>>> copy['right'] = 'privilege'
>>> opposites['right']
'left'
```

10.4 Sparse matrices

In Section 8.14, we used a list of lists to represent a matrix. That is a good choice for a matrix with mostly nonzero values, but consider a sparse matrix like this one:

$$\begin{bmatrix} 0 & 0 & 0 & 1 & 0 \\ 0 & 0 & 0 & 0 & 0 \\ 0 & 2 & 0 & 0 & 0 \\ 0 & 0 & 0 & 0 & 0 \\ 0 & 0 & 0 & 3 & 0 \end{bmatrix}$$

The list representation contains a lot of zeroes:

```
matrix = [ [0,0,0,1,0],
           [0,0,0,0,0],
           [0,2,0,0,0],
           [0,0,0,0,0],
           [0,0,0,3,0] ]
```

An alternative is to use a dictionary. For the keys, we can use tuples that contain the row and column numbers. Here is the dictionary representation of the same matrix:

```
matrix = {(0,3): 1, (2, 1): 2, (4, 3): 3}
```

We only need three key-value pairs, one for each nonzero element of the matrix. Each key is a tuple, and each value is an integer.

To access an element of the matrix, we could use the [] operator:

```
matrix[0,3]
1
```

Notice that the syntax for the dictionary representation is not the same as the syntax for the nested list representation. Instead of two integer indices, we use one index, which is a tuple of integers.

There is one problem. If we specify an element that is zero, we get an error, because there is no entry in the dictionary with that key:

```
>>> matrix[1,3]
KeyError: (1, 3)
```

The `get` method solves this problem:

```
>>> matrix.get((0,3), 0)
1
```

The first argument is the key; the second argument is the value `get` should return if the key is not in the dictionary:

```
>>> matrix.get((1,3), 0)
0
```

`get` definitely improves the semantics of accessing a sparse matrix. Shame about the syntax.

10.5 Hints

If you played around with the `fibonacci` function from Section 5.7, you might have noticed that the bigger the argument you provide, the longer the function takes to run. Furthermore, the run time increases very quickly. On one of our machines, `fibonacci(20)` finishes instantly, `fibonacci(30)` takes about a second, and `fibonacci(40)` takes roughly forever.

To understand why, consider this **call graph** for `fibonacci` with `n=4`:

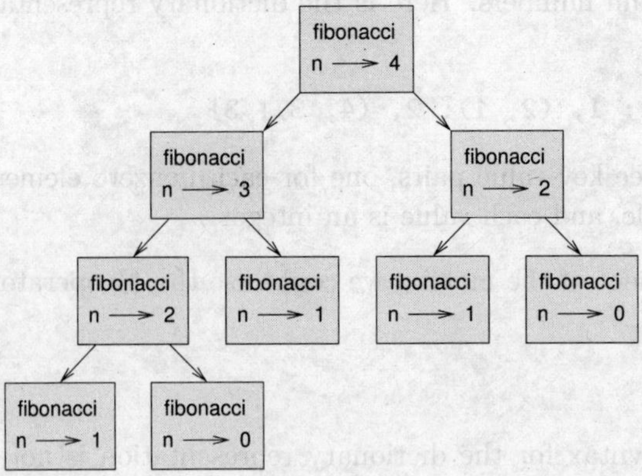

A call graph shows a set function frames, with lines connecting each frame to the frames of the functions it calls. At the top of the graph, `fibonacci` with `n=4` calls `fibonacci` with `n=3` and `n=2`. In turn, `fibonacci` with `n=3` calls `fibonacci` with `n=2` and `n=1`. And so on.

Count how many times `fibonacci(0)` and `fibonacci(1)` are called. This is an inefficient solution to the problem, and it gets far worse as the argument gets bigger.

A good solution is to keep track of values that have already been computed by storing them in a dictionary. A previously computed value that is stored for later use is called a **hint**. Here is an implementation of `fibonacci` using hints:

```
previous = {0:1, 1:1}

def fibonacci(n):
  if previous.has_key(n):
    return previous[n]
  else:
    newValue = fibonacci(n-1) + fibonacci(n-2)
    previous[n] = newValue
    return newValue
```

The dictionary named `previous` keeps track of the Fibonacci numbers we already know. We start with only two pairs: 0 maps to 1; and 1 maps to 1.

Whenever `fibonacci` is called, it checks the dictionary to determine if it contains the result. If it's there, the function can return immediately without making any more recursive calls. If not, it has to compute the new value. The new value is added to the dictionary before the function returns.

Using this version of `fibonacci`, our machines can compute `fibonacci(40)` in an eyeblink. But when we try to compute `fibonacci(50)`, we see the following:

```
>>> fibonacci(50)
20365011074L
```

The `L` at the end of the result indicates that the answer +(20,365,011,074) is too big to fit into a Python integer. Python has automatically converted the result to a long integer.

10.6 Long integers

Python provides a type called `long` that can handle any size integer. There are two ways to create a `long` value. One is to write an integer with a capital `L` at the end:

```
>>> type(1L)
<type 'long'>
```

The other is to use the `long` function to convert a value to a `long`. `long` can accept any numerical type and even strings of digits:

```
>>> long(1)
1L
>>> long(3.9)
3L
>>> long('57')
57L
```

All of the math operations work on `long`s, so in general any code that works with integers will also work with long integers. Any time the result of a computation is too big to be represented with an integer, Python detects the overflow and returns the result as a long integer. For example:

```
>>> 1000 * 1000
1000000
>>> 100000 * 100000
10000000000L
```

In the first case the result has type `int`; in the second case it is `long`.

10.7 Counting letters

In Chapter 7, we wrote a function that counted the number of occurrences of a letter in a string. A more general version of this problem is to form a histogram of the letters in the string, that is, how many times each letter appears.

Such a histogram might be useful for compressing a text file. Because different letters appear with different frequencies, we can compress a file by using shorter codes for common letters and longer codes for letters that appear less frequently.

Dictionaries provide an elegant way to generate a histogram:

```
>>> letterCounts = {}
>>> for letter in "Mississippi":
...     letterCounts[letter] = letterCounts.get (letter, 0) + 1
...
>>> letterCounts
{'M': 1, 's': 4, 'p': 2, 'i': 4}
```

We start with an empty dictionary. For each letter in the string, we find the current count (possibly zero) and increment it. At the end, the dictionary contains pairs of letters and their frequencies.

It might be more appealing to display the histogram in alphabetical order. We can do that with the `items` and `sort` methods:

```
>>> letterItems = letterCounts.items()
>>> letterItems.sort()
>>> print letterItems
[('M', 1), ('i', 4), ('p', 2), ('s', 4)]
```

You have seen the `items` method before, but `sort` is the first method you have encountered that applies to lists. There are several other list methods, including `append`, `extend`, and `reverse`. Consult the Python documentation for details.

10.8 Glossary

dictionary: A collection of key-value pairs that maps from keys to values. The keys can be any immutable type, and the values can be any type.

key: A value that is used to look up an entry in a dictionary.

key-value pair: One of the items in a dictionary.

method: A kind of function that is called with a different syntax and invoked "on" an object.

invoke: To call a method.

hint: Temporary storage of a precomputed value to avoid redundant computation.

overflow: A numerical result that is too large to be represented in a numerical format.

If there is no file named `test.dat`, it will be created. If there already is one, it will be replaced by the file we are writing.

When we print the file object, we see the name of the file, the mode, and the location of the object.

To put data in the file we invoke the `write` method on the file object:

```
>>> f.write("Now is the time")
>>> f.write("to close the file")
```

Closing the file tells the system that we are done writing and makes the file available for reading:

```
>>> f.close()
```

Now we can open the file again, this time for reading, and read the contents into a string. This time, the mode argument is `"r"` for reading:

```
>>> f = open("test.dat","r")
```

If we try to open a file that doesn't exist, we get an error:

```
>>> f = open("test.cat","r")
IOError: [Errno 2] No such file or directory: 'test.cat'
```

Not surprisingly, the `read` method reads data from the file. With no arguments, it reads the entire contents of the file:

```
>>> text = f.read()
>>> print text
Now is the timeto close the file
```

There is no space between "time" and "to" because we did not write a space between the strings.

`read` can also take an argument that indicates how many characters to read:

```
>>> f = open("test.dat","r")
>>> print f.read(5)
Now i
```

If not enough characters are left in the file, `read` returns the remaining characters. When we get to the end of the file, `read` returns the empty string:

```
>>> print f.read(1000006)
s the timeto close the file
>>> print f.read()

>>>
```

The following function copies a file, reading and writing up to fifty characters at a time. The first argument is the name of the original file; the second is the name of the new file:

```
def copyFile(oldFile, newFile):
  f1 = open(oldFile, "r")
  f2 = open(newFile, "w")
  while True:
    text = f1.read(50)
    if text == "":
      break
    f2.write(text)
  f1.close()
  f2.close()
  return
```

The `break` statement is new. Executing it breaks out of the loop; the flow of execution moves to the first statement after the loop.

In this example, the `while` loop is infinite because the value `True` is always true. The *only* way to get out of the loop is to execute `break`, which happens when `text` is the empty string, which happens when we get to the end of the file.

11.1 Text files

A **text file** is a file that contains printable characters and whitespace, organized into lines separated by newline characters. Since Python is specifically designed to process text files, it provides methods that make the job easy.

To demonstrate, we'll create a text file with three lines of text separated by newlines:

```
>>> f = open("test.dat","w")
>>> f.write("line one\nline two\nline three\n")
>>> f.close()
```

The `readline` method reads all the characters up to and including the next newline character:

```
>>> f = open("test.dat","r")
>>> print f.readline()
line one

>>>
```

This definition creates a new class called `Point`. The **pass** statement has no effect; it is only necessary because a compound statement must have something in its body.

By creating the `Point` class, we created a new type, also called `Point`. The members of this type are called **instances** of the type or **objects**. Creating a new instance is called **instantiation**. To instantiate a `Point` object, we call a function named (you guessed it) `Point`:

```
blank = Point()
```

The variable `blank` is assigned a reference to a new `Point` object. A function like `Point` that creates new objects is called a **constructor**.

12.2 Attributes

We can add new data to an instance using dot notation:

```
>>> blank.x = 3.0
>>> blank.y = 4.0
```

This syntax is similar to the syntax for selecting a variable from a module, such as `math.pi` or `string.uppercase`. In this case, though, we are selecting a data item from an instance. These named items are called **attributes**.

The following state diagram shows the result of these assignments:

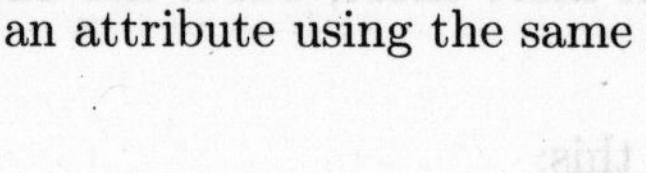

The variable `blank` refers to a Point object, which contains two attributes. Each attribute refers to a floating-point number.

We can read the value of an attribute using the same syntax:

```
>>> print blank.y
4.0
>>> x = blank.x
>>> print x
3.0
```

The expression `blank.x` means, "Go to the object `blank` refers to and get the value of `x`." In this case, we assign that value to a variable named `x`. There is no conflict between the variable x and the attribute x. The purpose of dot notation is to identify which variable you are referring to unambiguously.

You can use dot notation as part of any expression, so the following statements are legal:

```
print '(' + str(blank.x) + ', ' + str(blank.y) + ')'
distanceSquared = blank.x * blank.x + blank.y * blank.y
```

The first line outputs `(3.0, 4.0)`; the second line calculates the value 25.0.

You might be tempted to print the value of `blank` itself:

```
>>> print blank
<__main__.Point instance at 80f8e70>
```

The result indicates that `blank` is an instance of the `Point` class and it was defined in __main__. `80f8e70` is the unique identifier for this object, written in hexadecimal (base 16). This is probably not the most informative way to display a `Point` object. You will see how to change it shortly.

> *As an exercise, create and print a* `Point` *object, and then use* `id` *to print the object's unique identifier. Translate the hexadecimal form into decimal and confirm that they match.*

12.3 Instances as arguments

You can pass an instance as an argument in the usual way. For example:

```
def printPoint(p):
  print '(' + str(p.x) + ', ' + str(p.y) + ')'
```

`printPoint` takes a point as an argument and displays it in the standard format. If you call `printPoint(blank)`, the output is `(3.0, 4.0)`.

> *As an exercise, rewrite the* `distance` *function from Section 5.2 so that it takes two* `Point`*s as arguments instead of four numbers.*

12.4 Sameness

The meaning of the word "same" seems perfectly clear until you give it some thought, and then you realize there is more to it than you expected.

For example, if you say, "Chris and I have the same car," you mean that his car and yours are the same make and model, but that they are two different cars.

If you say, "Chris and I have the same mother," you mean that his mother and yours are the same person.[1] So the idea of "sameness" is different depending on the context.

When you talk about objects, there is a similar ambiguity. For example, if two Points are the same, does that mean they contain the same data (coordinates) or that they are actually the same object?

To find out if two references refer to the same object, use the is operator. For example:

```
>>> p1 = Point()
>>> p1.x = 3
>>> p1.y = 4
>>> p2 = Point()
>>> p2.x = 3
>>> p2.y = 4
>>> p1 is p2
False
```

Even though p1 and p2 contain the same coordinates, they are not the same object. If we assign p1 to p2, then the two variables are aliases of the same object:

```
>>> p2 = p1
>>> p1 is p2
True
```

This type of equality is called **shallow equality** because it compares only the references, not the contents of the objects.

To compare the contents of the objects—**deep equality**—we can write a function called samePoint:

```
def samePoint(p1, p2) :
  return (p1.x == p2.x) and (p1.y == p2.y)
```

Now if we create two different objects that contain the same data, we can use samePoint to find out if they represent the same point.

---

[1] Not all languages have the same problem. For example, German has different words for different kinds of sameness. "Same car" in this context would be "gleiche Auto," and "same mother" would be "selbe Mutter."

```
>>> p1 = Point()
>>> p1.x = 3
>>> p1.y = 4
>>> p2 = Point()
>>> p2.x = 3
>>> p2.y = 4
>>> samePoint(p1, p2)
True
```

Of course, if the two variables refer to the same object, they have both shallow and deep equality.

12.5 Rectangles

Let's say that we want a class to represent a rectangle. The question is, what information do we have to provide in order to specify a rectangle? To keep things simple, assume that the rectangle is oriented either vertically or horizontally, never at an angle.

There are a few possibilities: we could specify the center of the rectangle (two coordinates) and its size (width and height); or we could specify one of the corners and the size; or we could specify two opposing corners. A conventional choice is to specify the upper-left corner of the rectangle and the size.

Again, we'll define a new class:

```
class Rectangle:
  pass
```

And instantiate it:

```
box = Rectangle()
box.width = 100.0
box.height = 200.0
```

This code creates a new `Rectangle` object with two floating-point attributes. To specify the upper-left corner, we can embed an object within an object!

```
box.corner = Point()
box.corner.x = 0.0
box.corner.y = 0.0
```

The dot operator composes. The expression `box.corner.x` means, "Go to the object `box` refers to and select the attribute named `corner`; then go to that object and select the attribute named `x`."

The figure shows the state of this object:

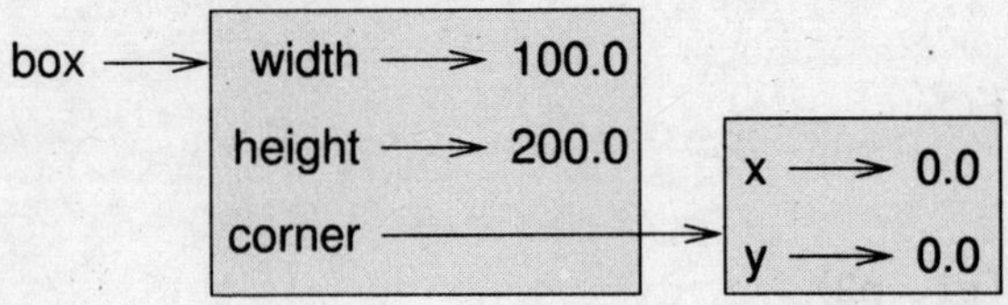

12.6 Instances as return values

Functions can return instances. For example, `findCenter` takes a `Rectangle` as an argument and returns a `Point` that contains the coordinates of the center of the `Rectangle`:

```
def findCenter(box):
  p = Point()
  p.x = box.corner.x + box.width/2.0
  p.y = box.corner.y - box.height/2.0
  return p
```

To call this function, pass `box` as an argument and assign the result to a variable:

```
>>> center = findCenter(box)
>>> printPoint(center)
(50.0, -100.0)
```

12.7 Objects are mutable

We can change the state of an object by making an assignment to one of its attributes. For example, to change the size of a rectangle without changing its position, we could modify the values of `width` and `height`:

```
box.width = box.width + 50
box.height = box.height + 100
```

We could encapsulate this code in a method and generalize it to grow the rectangle by any amount:

```
def growRect(box, dwidth, dheight) :
  box.width = box.width + dwidth
  box.height = box.height + dheight
```

The variables dwidth and dheight indicate how much the rectangle should grow in each direction. Invoking this method has the effect of modifying the Rectangle that is passed as an argument.

For example, we could create a new Rectangle named bob and pass it to growRect:

```
>>> bob = Rectangle()
>>> bob.width = 100.0
>>> bob.height = 200.0
>>> bob.corner = Point()
>>> bob.corner.x = 0.0
>>> bob.corner.y = 0.0
>>> growRect(bob, 50, 100)
```

While growRect is running, the parameter box is an alias for bob. Any changes made to box also affect bob.

> *As an exercise, write a function named* moveRect *that takes a* Rectangle *and two parameters named* dx *and* dy*. It should change the location of the rectangle by adding* dx *to the* x *coordinate of* corner *and adding* dy *to the* y *coordinate of* corner*.*

12.8 Copying

Aliasing can make a program difficult to read because changes made in one place might have unexpected effects in another place. It is hard to keep track of all the variables that might refer to a given object.

Copying an object is often an alternative to aliasing. The copy module contains a function called copy that can duplicate any object:

```
>>> import copy
>>> p1 = Point()
>>> p1.x = 3
>>> p1.y = 4
>>> p2 = copy.copy(p1)
>>> p1 == p2
False
>>> samePoint(p1, p2)
True
```

Once we import the copy module, we can use the copy method to make a new Point. p1 and p2 are not the same point, but they contain the same data.

To copy a simple object like a `Point`, which doesn't contain any embedded objects, `copy` is sufficient. This is called **shallow copying**.

For something like a `Rectangle`, which contains a reference to a `Point`, `copy` doesn't do quite the right thing. It copies the reference to the `Point` object, so both the old `Rectangle` and the new one refer to a single `Point`.

If we create a box, `b1`, in the usual way and then make a copy, `b2`, using `copy`, the resulting state diagram looks like this:

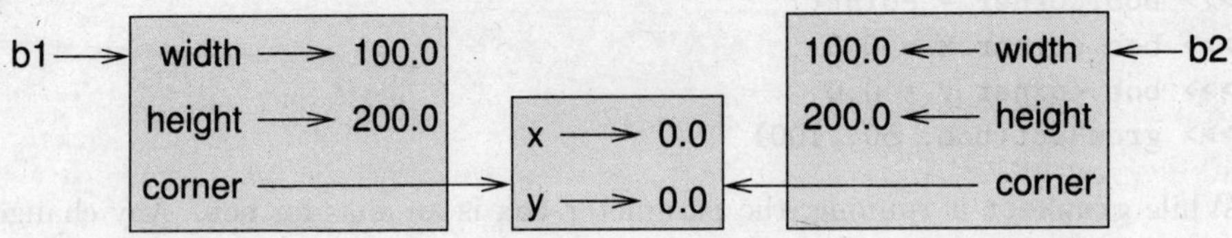

This is almost certainly not what we want. In this case, invoking `growRect` on one of the `Rectangles` would not affect the other, but invoking `moveRect` on either would affect both! This behavior is confusing and error-prone.

Fortunately, the `copy` module contains a method named `deepcopy` that copies not only the object but also any embedded objects. You will not be surprised to learn that this operation is called a **deep copy**.

```
>>> b2 = copy.deepcopy(b1)
```

Now `b1` and `b2` are completely separate objects.

We can use `deepcopy` to rewrite `growRect` so that instead of modifying an existing `Rectangle`, it creates a new `Rectangle` that has the same location as the old one but new dimensions:

```
def growRect(box, dwidth, dheight) :
  import copy
  newBox = copy.deepcopy(box)
  newBox.width = newBox.width + dwidth
  newBox.height = newBox.height + dheight
  return newBox
```

> *An an exercise, rewrite* `moveRect` *so that it creates and returns a new* `Rectangle` *instead of modifying the old one.*

12.9 Glossary

class: A user-defined compound type. A class can also be thought of as a template for the objects that are instances of it.

instantiate: To create an instance of a class.

instance: An object that belongs to a class.

object: A compound data type that is often used to model a thing or concept in the real world.

constructor: A method used to create new objects.

attribute: One of the named data items that makes up an instance.

shallow equality: Equality of references, or two references that point to the same object.

deep equality: Equality of values, or two references that point to objects that have the same value.

shallow copy: To copy the contents of an object, including any references to embedded objects; implemented by the `copy` function in the `copy` module.

deep copy: To copy the contents of an object as well as any embedded objects, and any objects embedded in them, and so on; implemented by the `deepcopy` function in the `copy` module.

12.9 Glossary

class: A user-defined compound type. A class can also be thought of as a template for the objects that are instances of it.

instantiate: To create an instance of a class.

instance: An object that belongs to a class.

object: A compound data type that is often used to model a thing or concept in the real world.

constructor: A method used to create new objects.

attribute: One of the named data items that makes up an instance.

shallow equality: Equality of references, or two references that point to the same object.

deep equality: Equality of values, or two references that point to objects that have the same value.

shallow copy: To copy the contents of an object, including any references to embedded objects; implemented by the copy function in the copy module.

deep copy: To copy the contents of an object as well as any embedded objects, and any objects embedded in them, and so on; implemented by the deepcopy function in the copy module.

Chapter 13

Classes and functions

13.1 Time

As another example of a user-defined type, we'll define a class called Time that records the time of day. The class definition looks like this:

```
class Time:
  pass
```

We can create a new Time object and assign attributes for hours, minutes, and seconds:

```
time = Time()
time.hours = 11
time.minutes = 59
time.seconds = 30
```

The state diagram for the Time object looks like this:

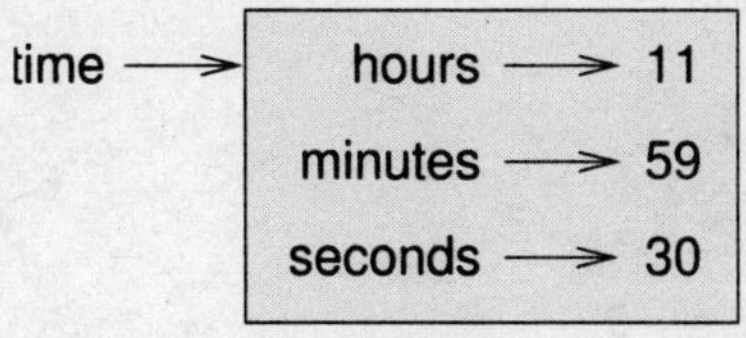

As an exercise, write a function `printTime` *that takes a* `Time` *object as an argument and prints it in the form* `hours:minutes:seconds`.

As a second exercise, write a boolean function `after` *that takes two* `Time` *objects,* `t1` *and* `t2`*, as arguments, and returns* `True` *if* `t1` *follows* `t2` *chronologically and* `False` *otherwise.*

13.2 Pure functions

In the next few sections, we'll write two versions of a function called `addTime`, which calculates the sum of two `Times`. They will demonstrate two kinds of functions: pure functions and modifiers.

The following is a rough version of `addTime`:

```
def addTime(t1, t2):
  sum = Time()
  sum.hours = t1.hours + t2.hours
  sum.minutes = t1.minutes + t2.minutes
  sum.seconds = t1.seconds + t2.seconds
  return sum
```

The function creates a new `Time` object, initializes its attributes, and returns a reference to the new object. This is called a **pure function** because it does not modify any of the objects passed to it as arguments and it has no side effects, such as displaying a value or getting user input.

Here is an example of how to use this function. We'll create two `Time` objects: `currentTime`, which contains the current time; and `breadTime`, which contains the amount of time it takes for a breadmaker to make bread. Then we'll use `addTime` to figure out when the bread will be done. If you haven't finished writing `printTime` yet, take a look ahead to Section 14.2 before you try this:

```
>>> currentTime = Time()
>>> currentTime.hours = 9
>>> currentTime.minutes = 14
>>> currentTime.seconds =  30

>>> breadTime = Time()
>>> breadTime.hours =  3
>>> breadTime.minutes = 35
>>> breadTime.seconds =  0

>>> doneTime = addTime(currentTime, breadTime)
>>> printTime(doneTime)
```

The output of this program is `12:49:30`, which is correct. On the other hand, there are cases where the result is not correct. Can you think of one?

The problem is that this function does not deal with cases where the number of seconds or minutes adds up to more than sixty. When that happens, we have to "carry" the extra seconds into the minutes column or the extra minutes into the hours column.

Here's a second corrected version of the function:

```
def addTime(t1, t2):
  sum = Time()
  sum.hours = t1.hours + t2.hours
  sum.minutes = t1.minutes + t2.minutes
  sum.seconds = t1.seconds + t2.seconds

  if sum.seconds >= 60:
    sum.seconds = sum.seconds - 60
    sum.minutes = sum.minutes + 1

  if sum.minutes >= 60:
    sum.minutes = sum.minutes - 60
    sum.hours = sum.hours + 1

  return sum
```

Although this function is correct, it is starting to get big. Later we will suggest an alternative approach that yields shorter code.

13.3 Modifiers

There are times when it is useful for a function to modify one or more of the objects it gets as arguments. Usually, the caller keeps a reference to the objects it passes, so any changes the function makes are visible to the caller. Functions that work this way are called **modifiers**.

`increment`, which adds a given number of seconds to a `Time` object, would be written most naturally as a modifier. A rough draft of the function looks like this:

```
def increment(time, seconds):
  time.seconds = time.seconds + seconds

  if time.seconds >= 60:
    time.seconds = time.seconds - 60
    time.minutes = time.minutes + 1

  if time.minutes >= 60:
    time.minutes = time.minutes - 60
    time.hours = time.hours + 1
```

The first line performs the basic operation; the remainder deals with the special cases we saw before.

Is this function correct? What happens if the parameter seconds is much greater than sixty? In that case, it is not enough to carry once; we have to keep doing it until seconds is less than sixty. One solution is to replace the if statements with while statements:

```
def increment(time, seconds):
  time.seconds = time.seconds + seconds

  while time.seconds >= 60:
    time.seconds = time.seconds - 60
    time.minutes = time.minutes + 1

  while time.minutes >= 60:
    time.minutes = time.minutes - 60
    time.hours = time.hours + 1
```

This function is now correct, but it is not the most efficient solution.

> *As an exercise, rewrite this function so that it doesn't contain any loops.*
>
> *As a second exercise, rewrite* increment *as a pure function, and write function calls to both versions.*

13.4 Which is better?

Anything that can be done with modifiers can also be done with pure functions. In fact, some programming languages only allow pure functions. There is some evidence that programs that use pure functions are faster to develop and less error-prone than programs that use modifiers. Nevertheless, modifiers are convenient at times, and in some cases, functional programs are less efficient.

In general, we recommend that you write pure functions whenever it is reasonable to do so and resort to modifiers only if there is a compelling advantage. This approach might be called a **functional programming style**.

13.5 Prototype development versus planning

In this chapter, we demonstrated an approach to program development that we call **prototype development**. In each case, we wrote a rough draft (or prototype) that performed the basic calculation and then tested it on a few cases, correcting flaws as we found them.

Although this approach can be effective, it can lead to code that is unnecessarily complicated—since it deals with many special cases—and unreliable—since it is hard to know if you have found all the errors.

An alternative is **planned development**, in which high-level insight into the problem can make the programming much easier. In this case, the insight is that a `Time` object is really a three-digit number in base 60! The `second` component is the "ones column," the `minute` component is the "sixties column," and the `hour` component is the "thirty-six hundreds column."

When we wrote `addTime` and `increment`, we were effectively doing addition in base 60, which is why we had to carry from one column to the next.

This observation suggests another approach to the whole problem—we can convert a `Time` object into a single number and take advantage of the fact that the computer knows how to do arithmetic with numbers. The following function converts a `Time` object into an integer:

```
def convertToSeconds(t):
  minutes = t.hours * 60 + t.minutes
  seconds = minutes * 60 + t.seconds
  return seconds
```

Now, all we need is a way to convert from an integer to a `Time` object:

```
def makeTime(seconds):
  time = Time()
  time.hours = seconds // 3600
  time.minutes = (seconds%3600) // 60
  time.seconds = seconds%60
  return time
```

You might have to think a bit to convince yourself that this function is correct. Assuming you are convinced, you can use it and `convertToSeconds` to rewrite `addTime`:

```
def addTime(t1, t2):
  seconds = convertToSeconds(t1) + convertToSeconds(t2)
  return makeTime(seconds)
```

This version is much shorter than the original, and it is much easier to demonstrate that it is correct.

As an exercise, rewrite `increment` *the same way.*

13.6 Generalization

In some ways, converting from base 60 to base 10 and back is harder than just dealing with times. Base conversion is more abstract; our intuition for dealing with times is better.

But if we have the insight to treat times as base 60 numbers and make the investment of writing the conversion functions (`convertToSeconds` and `makeTime`), we get a program that is shorter, easier to read and debug, and more reliable.

It is also easier to add features later. For example, imagine subtracting two `Times` to find the duration between them. The naïve approach would be to implement subtraction with borrowing. Using the conversion functions would be easier and more likely to be correct.

Ironically, sometimes making a problem harder (or more general) makes it easier (because there are fewer special cases and fewer opportunities for error).

13.7 Algorithms

When you write a general solution for a class of problems, as opposed to a specific solution to a single problem, you have written an **algorithm**. We mentioned this word before but did not define it carefully. It is not easy to define, so we will try a couple of approaches.

First, consider something that is not an algorithm. When you learned to multiply single-digit numbers, you probably memorized the multiplication table. In effect, you memorized 100 specific solutions. That kind of knowledge is not algorithmic.

But if you were "lazy," you probably cheated by learning a few tricks. For example, to find the product of n and 9, you can write $n-1$ as the first digit and $10-n$ as the second digit. This trick is a general solution for multiplying any single-digit number by 9. That's an algorithm!

Similarly, the techniques you learned for addition with carrying, subtraction with borrowing, and long division are all algorithms. One of the characteristics of algorithms is that they do not require any intelligence to carry out. They are mechanical processes in which each step follows from the last according to a simple set of rules.

In our opinion, it is embarrassing that humans spend so much time in school learning to execute algorithms that, quite literally, require no intelligence.

On the other hand, the process of designing algorithms is interesting, intellectually challenging, and a central part of what we call programming.

Some of the things that people do naturally, without difficulty or conscious thought, are the hardest to express algorithmically. Understanding natural language is a good example. We all do it, but so far no one has been able to explain *how* we do it, at least not in the form of an algorithm.

13.8 Glossary

pure function: A function that does not modify any of the objects it receives as arguments. Most pure functions are fruitful.

modifier: A function that changes one or more of the objects it receives as arguments. Most modifiers are fruitless.

functional programming style: A style of program design in which the majority of functions are pure.

prototype development: A way of developing programs starting with a prototype and gradually testing and improving it.

planned development: A way of developing programs that involves high-level insight into the problem and more planning than incremental development or prototype development.

algorithm: A set of instructions for solving a class of problems by a mechanical, unintelligent process.

Similarly, the techniques you learned for addition with carrying, subtraction with borrowing, and long division are all algorithms. One of the characteristics of algorithms is that they do not require any intelligence to carry out. They are mechanical processes in which each step follows from the last according to a simple set of rules.

In our opinion, it is embarrassing that humans spend so much time in school learning to execute algorithms that, quite literally, require no intelligence.

On the other hand, the process of designing algorithms is interesting, intellectually challenging, and a central part of what we call programming.

Some of the things that people do naturally, without difficulty or conscious thought, are the hardest to express algorithmically. Understanding natural language is a good example. We all do it, but so far no one has been able to explain how we do it, at least not in the form of an algorithm.

13.8 Glossary

pure function: A function that does not modify any of the objects it receives as arguments. Most pure functions are fruitful.

modifier: A function that changes one or more of the objects it receives as arguments. Most modifiers are fruitless.

functional programming style: A style of program design in which the majority of functions are pure.

prototype development: A way of developing programs starting with a prototype and gradually testing and improving it.

planned development: A way of developing programs that involves high-level insight into the problem and more planning than incremental development or prototype development.

algorithm: A set of instructions for solving a class of problems by a mechanical, unintelligent process.

Chapter 14

Classes and methods

14.1 Object-oriented features

Python is an **object-oriented programming language**, which means that it provides features that support **object-oriented programming**.

It is not easy to define object-oriented programming, but we have already seen some of its characteristics:

- Programs are made up of object definitions and function definitions, and most of the computation is expressed in terms of operations on objects.
- Each object definition corresponds to some object or concept in the real world, and the functions that operate on that object correspond to the ways real-world objects interact.

For example, the `Time` class defined in Chapter 13 corresponds to the way people record the time of day, and the functions we defined correspond to the kinds of things people do with times. Similarly, the `Point` and `Rectangle` classes correspond to the mathematical concepts of a point and a rectangle.

So far, we have not taken advantage of the features Python provides to support object-oriented programming. Strictly speaking, these features are not necessary. For the most part, they provide an alternative syntax for things we have already done, but in many cases, the alternative is more concise and more accurately conveys the structure of the program.

For example, in the `Time` program, there is no obvious connection between the class definition and the function definitions that follow. With some examination, it is apparent that every function takes at least one `Time` object as an argument.

This observation is the motivation for **methods**. We have already seen some methods, such as `keys` and `values`, which were invoked on dictionaries. Each method is associated with a class and is intended to be invoked on instances of that class.

Methods are just like functions, with two differences:

- Methods are defined inside a class definition in order to make the relationship between the class and the method explicit.
- The syntax for invoking a method is different from the syntax for calling a function.

In the next few sections, we will take the functions from the previous two chapters and transform them into methods. This transformation is purely mechanical; you can do it simply by following a sequence of steps. If you are comfortable converting from one form to another, you will be able to choose the best form for whatever you are doing.

14.2 printTime

In Chapter 13, we defined a class named `Time` and you wrote a function named `printTime`, which should have looked something like this:

```
class Time:
  pass

def printTime(time):
  print str(time.hours) + ":" + \
        str(time.minutes) + ":" + \
        str(time.seconds)
```

To call this function, we passed a `Time` object as an argument:

```
>>> currentTime = Time()
>>> currentTime.hours = 9
>>> currentTime.minutes = 14
>>> currentTime.seconds = 30
>>> printTime(currentTime)
```

To make `printTime` a method, all we have to do is move the function definition inside the class definition. Notice the change in indentation.

```
class Time:
  def printTime(time):
    print str(time.hours) + ":" +  \
          str(time.minutes) + ":" + \
          str(time.seconds)
```

Now we can invoke `printTime` using dot notation.

```
>>> currentTime.printTime()
```

As usual, the object on which the method is invoked appears before the dot and the name of the method appears after the dot.

The object on which the method is invoked is assigned to the first parameter, so in this case `currentTime` is assigned to the parameter `time`.

By convention, the first parameter of a method is called `self`. The reason for this is a little convoluted, but it is based on a useful metaphor.

The syntax for a function call, `printTime(currentTime)`, suggests that the function is the active agent. It says something like, "Hey `printTime`! Here's an object for you to print."

In object-oriented programming, the objects are the active agents. An invocation like `currentTime.printTime()` says "Hey `currentTime`! Please print yourself!"

This change in perspective might be more polite, but it is not obvious that it is useful. In the examples we have seen so far, it may not be. But sometimes shifting responsibility from the functions onto the objects makes it possible to write more versatile functions, and makes it easier to maintain and reuse code.

14.3 Another example

Let's convert `increment` (from Section 13.3) to a method. To save space, we will leave out previously defined methods, but you should keep them in your version:

```
class Time:
  #previous method definitions here...

  def increment(self, seconds):
    self.seconds = seconds + self.seconds

    while self.seconds >= 60:
      self.seconds = self.seconds - 60
```

```
      self.minutes = self.minutes + 1

    while self.minutes >= 60:
      self.minutes = self.minutes - 60
      self.hours = self.hours + 1
```

The transformation is purely mechanical—we move the method definition into the class definition and change the name of the first parameter.

Now we can invoke increment as a method.

```
currentTime.increment(500)
```

Again, the object on which the method is invoked gets assigned to the first parameter, self. The second parameter, seconds gets the value 500.

> *As an exercise, convert* convertToSeconds *(from Section 13.5) to a method in the* Time *class.*

14.4 A more complicated example

The after function is slightly more complicated because it operates on two Time objects, not just one. We can only convert one of the parameters to self; the other stays the same:

```
class Time:
  #previous method definitions here...

  def after(self, time2):
    if self.hour > time2.hour:
      return 1
    if self.hour < time2.hour:
      return 0

    if self.minute > time2.minute:
      return 1
    if self.minute < time2.minute:
      return 0

    if self.second > time2.second:
      return 1
    return 0
```

We invoke this method on one object and pass the other as an argument:

```
if doneTime.after(currentTime):
  print "The bread is not done yet."
```

You can almost read the invocation like English: "If the done-time is after the current-time, then..."

14.5 Optional arguments

We have seen built-in functions that take a variable number of arguments. For example, `string.find` can take two, three, or four arguments.

It is possible to write user-defined functions with optional argument lists. For example, we can upgrade our own version of `find` to do the same thing as `string.find`.

This is the original version from Section 7.7:

```
def find(str, ch):
  index = 0
  while index < len(str):
    if str[index] == ch:
      return index
    index = index + 1
  return -1
```

This is the new and improved version:

```
def find(str, ch, start=0):
  index = start
  while index < len(str):
    if str[index] == ch:
      return index
    index = index + 1
  return -1
```

The third parameter, `start`, is optional because a default value, `0`, is provided. If we invoke `find` with only two arguments, it uses the default value and starts from the beginning of the string:

```
>>> find("apple", "p")
1
```

If we provide a third argument, it **overrides** the default:

```
>>> find("apple", "p", 2)
2
>>> find("apple", "p", 3)
-1
```

> *As an exercise, add a fourth parameter,* `end`*, that specifies where to stop looking.*
>
> *Warning: This exercise is a bit tricky. The default value of* `end` *should be* `len(str)`*, but that doesn't work. The default values are evaluated when the function is defined, not when it is called. When* `find` *is defined,* `str` *doesn't exist yet, so you can't find its length.*

14.6 The initialization method

The **initialization method** is a special method that is invoked when an object is created. The name of this method is `__init__` (two underscore characters, followed by `init`, and then two more underscores). An initialization method for the `Time` class looks like this:

```
class Time:
  def __init__(self, hours=0, minutes=0, seconds=0):
    self.hours = hours
    self.minutes = minutes
    self.seconds = seconds
```

There is no conflict between the attribute `self.hours` and the parameter `hours`. Dot notation specifies which variable we are referring to.

When we invoke the `Time` constructor, the arguments we provide are passed along to `init`:

```
>>> currentTime = Time(9, 14, 30)
>>> currentTime.printTime()
9:14:30
```

Because the arguments are optional, we can omit them:

```
>>> currentTime = Time()
>>> currentTime.printTime()
0:0:0
```

Or provide only the first:

```
>>> currentTime = Time (9)
>>> currentTime.printTime()
9:0:0
```

Or the first two:

```
>>> currentTime = Time (9, 14)
>>> currentTime.printTime()
9:14:0
```

Finally, we can make assignments to a subset of the parameters by naming them explicitly:

```
>>> currentTime = Time(seconds = 30, hours = 9)
>>> currentTime.printTime()
9:0:30
```

14.7 Points revisited

Let's rewrite the `Point` class from Section 12.1 in a more object-oriented style:

```
class Point:
  def __init__(self, x=0, y=0):
    self.x = x
    self.y = y

  def __str__(self):
    return '(' + str(self.x) + ', ' + str(self.y) + ')'
```

The initialization method takes x and y values as optional parameters; the default for either parameter is 0.

The next method, `__str__`, returns a string representation of a `Point` object. If a class provides a method named `__str__`, it overrides the default behavior of the Python built-in `str` function.

```
>>> p = Point(3, 4)
>>> str(p)
'(3, 4)'
```

Printing a `Point` object implicitly invokes `__str__` on the object, so defining `__str__` also changes the behavior of `print`:

```
>>> p = Point(3, 4)
>>> print p
(3, 4)
```

When we write a new class, we almost always start by writing `__init__`, which makes it easier to instantiate objects, and `__str__`, which is almost always useful for debugging.

14.8 Operator overloading

Some languages make it possible to change the definition of the built-in operators when they are applied to user-defined types. This feature is called **operator overloading**. It is especially useful when defining new mathematical types.

For example, to override the addition operator `+`, we provide a method named `__add__`:

```
class Point:
  # previously defined methods here...

  def __add__(self, other):
    return Point(self.x + other.x, self.y + other.y)
```

As usual, the first parameter is the object on which the method is invoked. The second parameter is conveniently named `other` to distinguish it from `self`. To add two `Points`, we create and return a new `Point` that contains the sum of the x coordinates and the sum of the y coordinates.

Now, when we apply the `+` operator to `Point` objects, Python invokes `__add__`:

```
>>>   p1 = Point(3, 4)
>>>   p2 = Point(5, 7)
>>>   p3 = p1 + p2
>>>   print p3
(8, 11)
```

The expression `p1 + p2` is equivalent to `p1.__add__(p2)`, but obviously more elegant.

> *As an exercise, add a method* `__sub__(self, other)` *that overloads the subtraction operator, and try it out.*

There are several ways to override the behavior of the multiplication operator: by defining a method named `__mul__`, or `__rmul__`, or both.

If the left operand of `*` is a `Point`, Python invokes `__mul__`, which assumes that the other operand is also a `Point`. It computes the **dot product** of the two points, defined according to the rules of linear algebra:

```
def __mul__(self, other):
  return self.x * other.x + self.y * other.y
```

If the left operand of `*` is a primitive type and the right operand is a `Point`, Python invokes `__rmul__`, which performs **scalar multiplication**:

```
def __rmul__(self, other):
  return Point(other * self.x,  other * self.y)
```

The result is a new `Point` whose coordinates are a multiple of the original coordinates. If `other` is a type that cannot be multiplied by a floating-point number, then `__rmul__` will yield an error.

This example demonstrates both kinds of multiplication:

```
>>> p1 = Point(3, 4)
>>> p2 = Point(5, 7)
>>> print p1 * p2
43
>>> print 2 * p2
(10, 14)
```

What happens if we try to evaluate `p2 * 2`? Since the first operand is a `Point`, Python invokes `__mul__` with `2` as the second argument. Inside `__mul__`, the program tries to access the `x` coordinate of `other`, which fails because an integer has no attributes:

```
>>> print p2 * 2
AttributeError: 'int' object has no attribute 'x'
```

Unfortunately, the error message is a bit opaque. This example demonstrates some of the difficulties of object-oriented programming. Sometimes it is hard enough just to figure out what code is running.

For a more complete example of operator overloading, see Appendix B.

14.9 Polymorphism

Most of the methods we have written only work for a specific type. When you create a new object, you write methods that operate on that type.

But there are certain operations that you will want to apply to many types, such as the arithmetic operations in the previous sections. If many types support the same set of operations, you can write functions that work on any of those types.

For example, the multadd operation (which is common in linear algebra) takes three arguments; it multiplies the first two and then adds the third. We can write it in Python like this:

```
def multadd (x, y, z):
  return x * y + z
```

This method will work for any values of x and y that can be multiplied and for any value of z that can be added to the product.

We can invoke it with numeric values:

```
>>> multadd (3, 2, 1)
7
```

Or with Points:

```
>>> p1 = Point(3, 4)
>>> p2 = Point(5, 7)
>>> print multadd (2, p1, p2)
(11, 15)
>>> print multadd (p1, p2, 1)
44
```

In the first case, the Point is multiplied by a scalar and then added to another Point. In the second case, the dot product yields a numeric value, so the third argument also has to be a numeric value.

A function like this that can take arguments with different types is called **polymorphic**.

As another example, consider the method **frontAndBack**, which prints a list twice, forward and backward:

```
def frontAndBack(front):
  import copy
  back = copy.copy(front)
  back.reverse()
  print str(front) + str(back)
```

Because the reverse method is a modifier, we make a copy of the list before reversing it. That way, this method doesn't modify the list it gets as an argument.

Here's an example that applies frontAndBack to a list:

```
>>>   myList = [1, 2, 3, 4]
>>>   frontAndBack(myList)
[1, 2, 3, 4][4, 3, 2, 1]
```

Of course, we intended to apply this function to lists, so it is not surprising that it works. What would be surprising is if we could apply it to a `Point`.

To determine whether a function can be applied to a new type, we apply the fundamental rule of polymorphism:

> **If all of the operations inside the function can be applied to the type, the function can be applied to the type.**

The operations in the method include `copy`, `reverse`, and `print`.

`copy` works on any object, and we have already written a `__str__` method for `Points`, so all we need is a `reverse` method in the `Point` class:

```
def reverse(self):
  self.x , self.y = self.y, self.x
```

Then we can pass `Points` to `frontAndBack`:

```
>>>   p = Point(3, 4)
>>>   frontAndBack(p)
(3, 4)(4, 3)
```

The best kind of polymorphism is the unintentional kind, where you discover that a function you have already written can be applied to a type for which you never planned.

14.10 Glossary

object-oriented language: A language that provides features, such as user-defined classes and inheritance, that facilitate object-oriented programming.

object-oriented programming: A style of programming in which data and the operations that manipulate it are organized into classes and methods.

method: A function that is defined inside a class definition and is invoked on instances of that class.

override: To replace a default. Examples include replacing a default value with a particular argument and replacing a default method by providing a new method with the same name.

initialization method: A special method that is invoked automatically when a new object is created and that initializes the object's attributes.

operator overloading: Extending built-in operators (+, -, *, >, <, etc.) so that they work with user-defined types.

dot product: An operation defined in linear algebra that multiplies two `Points` and yields a numeric value.

scalar multiplication: An operation defined in linear algebra that multiplies each of the coordinates of a `Point` by a numeric value.

polymorphic: A function that can operate on more than one type. If all the operations in a function can be applied to a type, then the function can be applied to a type.

Chapter 15

Sets of objects

15.1 Composition

By now, you have seen several examples of composition. One of the first examples was using a method invocation as part of an expression. Another example is the nested structure of statements; you can put an `if` statement within a `while` loop, within another `if` statement, and so on.

Having seen this pattern, and having learned about lists and objects, you should not be surprised to learn that you can create lists of objects. You can also create objects that contain lists (as attributes); you can create lists that contain lists; you can create objects that contain objects; and so on.

In this chapter and the next, we will look at some examples of these combinations, using `Card` objects as an example.

15.2 `Card` objects

If you are not familiar with common playing cards, now would be a good time to get a deck, or else this chapter might not make much sense. There are fifty-two cards in a deck, each of which belongs to one of four suits and one of thirteen ranks. The suits are Spades, Hearts, Diamonds, and Clubs (in descending order in bridge). The ranks are Ace, 2, 3, 4, 5, 6, 7, 8, 9, 10, Jack, Queen, and King. Depending on the game that you are playing, the rank of Ace may be higher than King or lower than 2.

If we want to define a new object to represent a playing card, it is obvious what the attributes should be: `rank` and `suit`. It is not as obvious what type the attributes should be. One possibility is to use strings containing words like "Spade" for suits and "Queen" for ranks. One problem with this implementation is that it would not be easy to compare cards to see which had a higher rank or suit.

An alternative is to use integers to **encode** the ranks and suits. By "encode," we do not mean what some people think, which is to encrypt or translate into a secret code. What a computer scientist means by "encode" is "to define a mapping between a sequence of numbers and the items I want to represent." For example:

Spades	$\mapsto$	3
Hearts	$\mapsto$	2
Diamonds	$\mapsto$	1
Clubs	$\mapsto$	0

An obvious feature of this mapping is that the suits map to integers in order, so we can compare suits by comparing integers. The mapping for ranks is fairly obvious; each of the numerical ranks maps to the corresponding integer, and for face cards:

Jack	$\mapsto$	11
Queen	$\mapsto$	12
King	$\mapsto$	13

The reason we are using mathematical notation for these mappings is that they are not part of the Python program. They are part of the program design, but they never appear explicitly in the code. The class definition for the Card type looks like this:

```
class Card:
  def __init__(self, suit=0, rank=2):
    self.suit = suit
    self.rank = rank
```

As usual, we provide an initialization method that takes an optional parameter for each attribute. The default value of suit is 0, which represents Clubs.

To create a Card, we invoke the Card constructor with the suit and rank of the card we want.

```
threeOfClubs = Card(3, 1)
```

In the next section we'll figure out which card we just made.

15.3 Class attributes and the __str__ method

In order to print Card objects in a way that people can easily read, we want to map the integer codes onto words. A natural way to do that is with lists of strings. We assign these lists to **class attributes** at the top of the class definition:

```
class Card:
  suitList = ["Clubs", "Diamonds", "Hearts", "Spades"]
  rankList = ["narf", "Ace", "2", "3", "4", "5", "6", "7",
              "8", "9", "10", "Jack", "Queen", "King"]

  #init method omitted

  def __str__(self):
    return (self.rankList[self.rank] + " of " +
            self.suitList[self.suit])
```

A class attribute is defined outside of any method, and it can be accessed from any of the methods in the class.

Inside __str__, we can use suitList and rankList to map the numerical values of suit and rank to strings. For example, the expression self.suitList[self.suit] means "use the attribute suit from the object self as an index into the class attribute named suitList, and select the appropriate string."

The reason for the "narf" in the first element in rankList is to act as a place keeper for the zero-eth element of the list, which should never be used. The only valid ranks are 1 to 13. This wasted item is not entirely necessary. We could have started at 0, as usual, but it is less confusing to encode 2 as 2, 3 as 3, and so on.

With the methods we have so far, we can create and print cards:

```
>>> card1 = Card(1, 11)
>>> print card1
Jack of Diamonds
```

Class attributes like suitList are shared by all Card objects. The advantage of this is that we can use any Card object to access the class attributes:

```
>>> card2 = Card(1, 3)
>>> print card2
3 of Diamonds
>>> print card2.suitList[1]
Diamonds
```

The disadvantage is that if we modify a class attribute, it affects every instance of the class. For example, if we decide that "Jack of Diamonds" should really be called "Jack of Swirly Whales," we could do this:

```
>>> card1.suitList[1] = "Swirly Whales"
>>> print card1
Jack of Swirly Whales
```

The problem is that *all* of the Diamonds just became Swirly Whales:

```
>>> print card2
3 of Swirly Whales
```

It is usually not a good idea to modify class attributes.

15.4 Comparing cards

For primitive types, there are conditional operators (<, >, ==, etc.) that compare values and determine when one is greater than, less than, or equal to another. For user-defined types, we can override the behavior of the built-in operators by providing a method named `__cmp__`. By convention, `__cmp__` has two parameters, `self` and `other`, and returns 1 if the first object is greater, -1 if the second object is greater, and 0 if they are equal to each other.

Some types are completely ordered, which means that you can compare any two elements and tell which is bigger. For example, the integers and the floating-point numbers are completely ordered. Some sets are unordered, which means that there is no meaningful way to say that one element is bigger than another. For example, the fruits are unordered, which is why you cannot compare apples and oranges.

The set of playing cards is partially ordered, which means that sometimes you can compare cards and sometimes not. For example, you know that the 3 of Clubs is higher than the 2 of Clubs, and the 3 of Diamonds is higher than the 3 of Clubs. But which is better, the 3 of Clubs or the 2 of Diamonds? One has a higher rank, but the other has a higher suit.

In order to make cards comparable, you have to decide which is more important, rank or suit. To be honest, the choice is arbitrary. For the sake of choosing, we will say that suit is more important, because a new deck of cards comes sorted with all the Clubs together, followed by all the Diamonds, and so on.

With that decided, we can write `__cmp__`:

```
def __cmp__(self, other):
  # check the suits
  if self.suit > other.suit: return 1
  if self.suit < other.suit: return -1
  # suits are the same... check ranks
  if self.rank > other.rank: return 1
  if self.rank < other.rank: return -1
  # ranks are the same... it's a tie
  return 0
```

In this ordering, Aces appear lower than Deuces (2s).

> *As an exercise, modify* `__cmp__` *so that Aces are ranked higher than Kings.*

15.5 Decks

Now that we have objects to represent `Cards`, the next logical step is to define a class to represent a `Deck`. Of course, a deck is made up of cards, so each `Deck` object will contain a list of cards as an attribute.

The following is a class definition for the `Deck` class. The initialization method creates the attribute `cards` and generates the standard set of fifty-two cards:

```
class Deck:
  def __init__(self):
    self.cards = []
    for suit in range(4):
      for rank in range(1, 14):
        self.cards.append(Card(suit, rank))
```

The easiest way to populate the deck is with a nested loop. The outer loop enumerates the suits from 0 to 3. The inner loop enumerates the ranks from 1 to 13. Since the outer loop iterates four times, and the inner loop iterates thirteen times, the total number of times the body is executed is fifty-two (thirteen times four). Each iteration creates a new instance of `Card` with the current suit and rank, and appends that card to the `cards` list.

The `append` method works on lists but not, of course, tuples.

15.6 Printing the deck

As usual, when we define a new type of object we want a method that prints the contents of an object. To print a `Deck`, we traverse the list and print each `Card`:

```
class Deck:
  ...
  def printDeck(self):
    for card in self.cards:
      print card
```

Here, and from now on, the ellipsis (...) indicates that we have omitted the other methods in the class.

As an alternative to printDeck, we could write a __str__ method for the Deck class. The advantage of __str__ is that it is more flexible. Rather than just printing the contents of the object, it generates a string representation that other parts of the program can manipulate before printing, or store for later use.

Here is a version of __str__ that returns a string representation of a Deck. To add a bit of pizzazz, it arranges the cards in a cascade where each card is indented one space more than the previous card:

```
class Deck:
  ...
  def __str__(self):
    s = ""
    for i in range(len(self.cards)):
      s = s + " "*i + str(self.cards[i]) + "\n"
    return s
```

This example demonstrates several features. First, instead of traversing self.cards and assigning each card to a variable, we are using i as a loop variable and an index into the list of cards.

Second, we are using the string multiplication operator to indent each card by one more space than the last. The expression " "*i yields a number of spaces equal to the current value of i.

Third, instead of using the print command to print the cards, we use the str function. Passing an object as an argument to str is equivalent to invoking the __str__ method on the object.

Finally, we are using the variable s as an **accumulator**. Initially, s is the empty string. Each time through the loop, a new string is generated and concatenated with the old value of s to get the new value. When the loop ends, s contains the complete string representation of the Deck, which looks like this:

```
>>> deck = Deck()
>>> print deck
Ace of Clubs
 2 of Clubs
  3 of Clubs
   4 of Clubs
    5 of Clubs
     6 of Clubs
      7 of Clubs
       8 of Clubs
        9 of Clubs
         10 of Clubs
          Jack of Clubs
           Queen of Clubs
            King of Clubs
             Ace of Diamonds
```

And so on. Even though the result appears on 52 lines, it is one long string that contains newlines.

15.7 Shuffling the deck

If a deck is perfectly shuffled, then any card is equally likely to appear anywhere in the deck, and any location in the deck is equally likely to contain any card.

To shuffle the deck, we will use the **randrange** function from the **random** module. With two integer arguments, a and b, **randrange** chooses a random integer in the range `a <= x < b`. Since the upper bound is strictly less than b, we can use the length of a list as the second argument, and we are guaranteed to get a legal index. For example, this expression chooses the index of a random card in a deck:

```
random.randrange(0, len(self.cards))
```

An easy way to shuffle the deck is by traversing the cards and swapping each card with a randomly chosen one. It is possible that the card will be swapped with itself, but that is fine. In fact, if we precluded that possibility, the order of the cards would be less than entirely random:

```
class Deck:
  ...
  def shuffle(self):
    import random
    nCards = len(self.cards)
    for i in range(nCards):
      j = random.randrange(i, nCards)
      self.cards[i], self.cards[j] = self.cards[j], self.cards[i]
```

Rather than assume that there are fifty-two cards in the deck, we get the actual length of the list and store it in `nCards`.

For each card in the deck, we choose a random card from among the cards that haven't been shuffled yet. Then we swap the current card (`i`) with the selected card (`j`). To swap the cards we use a tuple assignment, as in Section 9.2:

```
self.cards[i], self.cards[j] = self.cards[j], self.cards[i]
```

> *As an exercise, rewrite this line of code without using a sequence assignment.*

15.8 Removing and dealing cards

Another method that would be useful for the `Deck` class is `removeCard`, which takes a card as an argument, removes it, and returns `True` if the card was in the deck and `False` otherwise:

```
class Deck:
  ...
  def removeCard(self, card):
    if card in self.cards:
      self.cards.remove(card)
      return True
    else:
      return False
```

The `in` operator returns true if the first operand is in the second, which must be a list or a tuple. If the first operand is an object, Python uses the object's `__cmp__` method to determine equality with items in the list. Since the `__cmp__` in the `Card` class checks for deep equality, the `removeCard` method checks for deep equality.

To deal cards, we want to remove and return the top card. The list method `pop` provides a convenient way to do that:

```
class Deck:
  ...
  def popCard(self):
    return self.cards.pop()
```

Actually, pop removes the *last* card in the list, so we are in effect dealing from the bottom of the deck.

One more operation that we are likely to want is the boolean function `isEmpty`, which returns true if the deck contains no cards:

```
class Deck:
  ...
  def isEmpty(self):
    return (len(self.cards) == 0)
```

15.9 Glossary

encode: To represent one set of values using another set of values by constructing a mapping between them.

class attribute: A variable that is defined inside a class definition but outside any method. Class attributes are accessible from any method in the class and are shared by all instances of the class.

accumulator: A variable used in a loop to accumulate a series of values, such as by concatenating them onto a string or adding them to a running sum.

```
class Deck:
  ...
  def popCard(self):
    return self.cards.pop()
```

Actually, pop removes the *last* card in the list, so we are in effect dealing from the bottom of the deck.

One more operation that we are likely to want is the boolean function isEmpty, which returns true if the deck contains no cards:

```
class Deck:
  ...
  def isEmpty(self):
    return (len(self.cards) == 0)
```

15.9 Glossary

encode: To represent one set of values using another set of values by constructing a mapping between them.

class attribute: A variable that is defined inside a class definition but outside any method. Class attributes are accessible from any method in the class and are shared by all instances of the class.

accumulator: A variable used in a loop to accumulate a series of values, such as by concatenating them onto a string or adding them to a running sum.

Chapter 16

Inheritance

16.1 Inheritance

The language feature most often associated with object-oriented programming is **inheritance**. Inheritance is the ability to define a new class that is a modified version of an existing class.

The primary advantage of this feature is that you can add new methods to a class without modifying the existing class. It is called "inheritance" because the new class inherits all of the methods of the existing class. Extending this metaphor, the existing class is sometimes called the **parent** class. The new class may be called the **child** class or sometimes "subclass."

Inheritance is a powerful feature. Some programs that would be complicated without inheritance can be written concisely and simply with it. Also, inheritance can facilitate code reuse, since you can customize the behavior of parent classes without having to modify them. In some cases, the inheritance structure reflects the natural structure of the problem, which makes the program easier to understand.

On the other hand, inheritance can make programs difficult to read. When a method is invoked, it is sometimes not clear where to find its definition. The relevant code may be scattered among several modules. Also, many of the things that can be done using inheritance can be done as elegantly (or more so) without it. If the natural structure of the problem does not lend itself to inheritance, this style of programming can do more harm than good.

In this chapter we will demonstrate the use of inheritance as part of a program that plays the card game Old Maid. One of our goals is to write code that could be reused to implement other card games.

16.2 A hand of cards

For almost any card game, we need to represent a hand of cards. A hand is similar to a deck, of course. Both are made up of a set of cards, and both require operations like adding and removing cards. Also, we might like the ability to shuffle both decks and hands.

A hand is also different from a deck. Depending on the game being played, we might want to perform some operations on hands that don't make sense for a deck. For example, in poker we might classify a hand (straight, flush, etc.) or compare it with another hand. In bridge, we might want to compute a score for a hand in order to make a bid.

This situation suggests the use of inheritance. If `Hand` is a subclass of `Deck`, it will have all the methods of `Deck`, and new methods can be added.

In the class definition, the name of the parent class appears in parentheses:

```
class Hand(Deck):
  pass
```

This statement indicates that the new `Hand` class inherits from the existing `Deck` class.

The `Hand` constructor initializes the attributes for the hand, which are `name` and `cards`. The string `name` identifies this hand, probably by the name of the player that holds it. The name is an optional parameter with the empty string as a default value. `cards` is the list of cards in the hand, initialized to the empty list:

```
class Hand(Deck):
  def __init__(self, name=""):
    self.cards = []
    self.name = name
```

For just about any card game, it is necessary to add and remove cards from the deck. Removing cards is already taken care of, since `Hand` inherits `removeCard` from `Deck`. But we have to write `addCard`:

```
class Hand(Deck):
  ...
  def addCard(self,card) :
    self.cards.append(card)
```

Again, the ellipsis indicates that we have omitted other methods. The list `append` method adds the new card to the end of the list of cards.

16.3 Dealing cards

Now that we have a Hand class, we want to deal cards from the Deck into hands. It is not immediately obvious whether this method should go in the Hand class or in the Deck class, but since it operates on a single deck and (possibly) several hands, it is more natural to put it in Deck.

deal should be fairly general, since different games will have different requirements. We may want to deal out the entire deck at once or add one card to each hand.

deal takes three parameters: the deck, a list (or tuple) of hands, and the total number of cards to deal. If there are not enough cards in the deck, the method deals out all of the cards and stops:

```
class Deck :
  ...
  def deal(self, hands, nCards=999):
    nHands = len(hands)
    for i in range(nCards):
      if self.isEmpty(): break     # break if out of cards
      card = self.popCard()        # take the top card
      hand = hands[i % nHands]     # whose turn is next?
      hand.addCard(card)           # add the card to the hand
```

The last parameter, nCards, is optional; the default is a large number, which effectively means that all of the cards in the deck will get dealt.

The loop variable i goes from 0 to nCards-1. Each time through the loop, a card is removed from the deck using the list method pop, which removes and returns the last item in the list.

The modulus operator (%) allows us to deal cards in a round robin (one card at a time to each hand). When i is equal to the number of hands in the list, the expression i % nHands wraps around to the beginning of the list (index 0).

16.4 Printing a Hand

To print the contents of a hand, we can take advantage of the printDeck and __str__ methods inherited from Deck. For example:

```
>>> deck = Deck()
>>> deck.shuffle()
>>> hand = Hand("frank")
>>> deck.deal([hand], 5)
>>> print hand
Hand frank contains
2 of Spades
 3 of Spades
  4 of Spades
   Ace of Hearts
    9 of Clubs
```

It's not a great hand, but it has the makings of a straight flush.

Although it is convenient to inherit the existing methods, there is additional information in a Hand object we might want to include when we print one. To do that, we can provide a __str__ method in the Hand class that overrides the one in the Deck class:

```
class Hand(Deck)
  ...
  def __str__(self):
    s = "Hand " + self.name
    if self.isEmpty():
      return s + " is empty\n"
    else:
      return s + " contains\n" + Deck.__str__(self)
```

Initially, s is a string that identifies the hand. If the hand is empty, the program appends the words is empty and returns the result.

Otherwise, the program appends the word contains and the string representation of the Deck, computed by invoking the __str__ method in the Deck class on self.

It may seem odd to send self, which refers to the current Hand, to a Deck method, until you remember that a Hand is a kind of Deck. Hand objects can do everything Deck objects can, so it is legal to send a Hand to a Deck method.

In general, it is always legal to use an instance of a subclass in place of an instance of a parent class.

16.5 The CardGame class

The CardGame class takes care of some basic chores common to all games, such as creating the deck and shuffling it:

```
class CardGame:
  def __init__(self):
    self.deck = Deck()
    self.deck.shuffle()
```

This is the first case we have seen where the initialization method performs a significant computation, beyond initializing attributes.

To implement specific games, we can inherit from `CardGame` and add features for the new game. As an example, we'll write a simulation of Old Maid.

The object of Old Maid is to get rid of cards in your hand. You do this by matching cards by rank and color. For example, the 4 of Clubs matches the 4 of Spades since both suits are black. The Jack of Hearts matches the Jack of Diamonds since both are red.

To begin the game, the Queen of Clubs is removed from the deck so that the Queen of Spades has no match. The fifty-one remaining cards are dealt to the players in a round robin. After the deal, all players match and discard as many cards as possible.

When no more matches can be made, play begins. In turn, each player picks a card (without looking) from the closest neighbor to the left who still has cards. If the chosen card matches a card in the player's hand, the pair is removed. Otherwise, the card is added to the player's hand. Eventually all possible matches are made, leaving only the Queen of Spades in the loser's hand.

In our computer simulation of the game, the computer plays all hands. Unfortunately, some nuances of the real game are lost. In a real game, the player with the Old Maid goes to some effort to get their neighbor to pick that card, by displaying it a little more prominently, or perhaps failing to display it more prominently, or even failing to fail to display that card more prominently. The computer simply picks a neighbor's card at random.

16.6 OldMaidHand class

A hand for playing Old Maid requires some abilities beyond the general abilities of a `Hand`. We will define a new class, `OldMaidHand`, that inherits from `Hand` and provides an additional method called `removeMatches`:

```
class OldMaidHand(Hand):
  def removeMatches(self):
    count = 0
    originalCards = self.cards[:]
```

```
  for card in originalCards:
    match = Card(3 - card.suit, card.rank)
    if match in self.cards:
      self.cards.remove(card)
      self.cards.remove(match)
      print "Hand %s: %s matches %s" % (self.name,card,match)
      count = count + 1
  return count
```

We start by making a copy of the list of cards, so that we can traverse the copy while removing cards from the original. Since `self.cards` is modified in the loop, we don't want to use it to control the traversal. Python can get quite confused if it is traversing a list that is changing!

For each card in the hand, we figure out what the matching card is and go looking for it. The match card has the same rank and the other suit of the same color. The expression `3 - card.suit` turns a Club (suit 0) into a Spade (suit 3) and a Diamond (suit 1) into a Heart (suit 2). You should satisfy yourself that the opposite operations also work. If the match card is also in the hand, both cards are removed.

The following example demonstrates how to use `removeMatches`:

```
>>> game = CardGame()
>>> hand = OldMaidHand("frank")
>>> game.deck.deal([hand], 13)
>>> print hand
Hand frank contains
Ace of Spades
 2 of Diamonds
  7 of Spades
   8 of Clubs
    6 of Hearts
     8 of Spades
      7 of Clubs
       Queen of Clubs
        7 of Diamonds
         5 of Clubs
          Jack of Diamonds
           10 of Diamonds
            10 of Hearts

>>> hand.removeMatches()
Hand frank: 7 of Spades matches 7 of Clubs
Hand frank: 8 of Spades matches 8 of Clubs
```

```
Hand frank: 10 of Diamonds matches 10 of Hearts
>>> print hand
Hand frank contains
Ace of Spades
 2 of Diamonds
  6 of Hearts
   Queen of Clubs
    7 of Diamonds
     5 of Clubs
      Jack of Diamonds
```

Notice that there is no __init__ method for the OldMaidHand class. We inherit it from Hand.

16.7 OldMaidGame class

Now we can turn our attention to the game itself. OldMaidGame is a subclass of CardGame with a new method called play that takes a list of players as an argument.

Since __init__ is inherited from CardGame, a new OldMaidGame object contains a new shuffled deck:

```
class OldMaidGame(CardGame):
  def play(self, names):
    # remove Queen of Clubs
    self.deck.removeCard(Card(0,12))

    # make a hand for each player
    self.hands = []
    for name in names :
      self.hands.append(OldMaidHand(name))

    # deal the cards
    self.deck.deal(self.hands)
    print "---------- Cards have been dealt"
    self.printHands()

    # remove initial matches
    matches = self.removeAllMatches()
    print "---------- Matches discarded, play begins"
    self.printHands()
```

```
    # play until all 50 cards are matched
    turn = 0
    numHands = len(self.hands)
    while matches < 25:
      matches = matches + self.playOneTurn(turn)
      turn = (turn + 1) % numHands

    print "---------- Game is Over"
    self.printHands()
```

Some of the steps of the game have been separated into methods. `removeAllMatches` traverses the list of hands and invokes `removeMatches` on each:

```
class OldMaidGame(CardGame):
  ...
  def removeAllMatches(self):
    count = 0
    for hand in self.hands:
      count = count + hand.removeMatches()
    return count
```

> *As an exercise, write* `printHands` *which traverses* `self.hands` *and prints each hand.*

`count` is an accumulator that adds up the number of matches in each hand and returns the total.

When the total number of matches reaches twenty-five, fifty cards have been removed from the hands, which means that only one card is left and the game is over.

The variable `turn` keeps track of which player's turn it is. It starts at 0 and increases by one each time; when it reaches `numHands`, the modulus operator wraps it back around to 0.

The method `playOneTurn` takes an argument that indicates whose turn it is. The return value is the number of matches made during this turn:

```
class OldMaidGame(CardGame):
  ...
  def playOneTurn(self, i):
    if self.hands[i].isEmpty():
      return 0
    neighbor = self.findNeighbor(i)
    pickedCard = self.hands[neighbor].popCard()
    self.hands[i].addCard(pickedCard)
    print "Hand", self.hands[i].name, "picked", pickedCard
    count = self.hands[i].removeMatches()
    self.hands[i].shuffle()
    return count
```

If a player's hand is empty, that player is out of the game, so he or she does nothing and returns 0.

Otherwise, a turn consists of finding the first player on the left that has cards, taking one card from the neighbor, and checking for matches. Before returning, the cards in the hand are shuffled so that the next player's choice is random.

The method `findNeighbor` starts with the player to the immediate left and continues around the circle until it finds a player that still has cards:

```
class OldMaidGame(CardGame):
  ...
  def findNeighbor(self, i):
    numHands = len(self.hands)
    for next in range(1,numHands):
      neighbor = (i + next) % numHands
      if not self.hands[neighbor].isEmpty():
        return neighbor
```

If `findNeighbor` ever went all the way around the circle without finding cards, it would return `None` and cause an error elsewhere in the program. Fortunately, we can prove that that will never happen (as long as the end of the game is detected correctly).

We have omitted the `printHands` method. You can write that one yourself.

The following output is from a truncated form of the game where only the top fifteen cards (tens and higher) were dealt to three players. With this small deck, play stops after seven matches instead of twenty-five.

```
>>> import cards
>>> game = cards.OldMaidGame()
>>> game.play(["Allen","Jeff","Chris"])
```

```
---------- Cards have been dealt
Hand Allen contains
King of Hearts
 Jack of Clubs
  Queen of Spades
   King of Spades
    10 of Diamonds

Hand Jeff contains
Queen of Hearts
 Jack of Spades
  Jack of Hearts
   King of Diamonds
    Queen of Diamonds

Hand Chris contains
Jack of Diamonds
 King of Clubs
  10 of Spades
   10 of Hearts
    10 of Clubs

Hand Jeff: Queen of Hearts matches Queen of Diamonds
Hand Chris: 10 of Spades matches 10 of Clubs
---------- Matches discarded, play begins
Hand Allen contains
King of Hearts
 Jack of Clubs
  Queen of Spades
   King of Spades
    10 of Diamonds

Hand Jeff contains
Jack of Spades
 Jack of Hearts
  King of Diamonds

Hand Chris contains
Jack of Diamonds
 King of Clubs
  10 of Hearts
```

```
Hand Allen picked King of Diamonds
Hand Allen: King of Hearts matches King of Diamonds
Hand Jeff picked 10 of Hearts
Hand Chris picked Jack of Clubs
Hand Allen picked Jack of Hearts
Hand Jeff picked Jack of Diamonds
Hand Chris picked Queen of Spades
Hand Allen picked Jack of Diamonds
Hand Allen: Jack of Hearts matches Jack of Diamonds
Hand Jeff picked King of Clubs
Hand Chris picked King of Spades
Hand Allen picked 10 of Hearts
Hand Allen: 10 of Diamonds matches 10 of Hearts
Hand Jeff picked Queen of Spades
Hand Chris picked Jack of Spades
Hand Chris: Jack of Clubs matches Jack of Spades
Hand Jeff picked King of Spades
Hand Jeff: King of Clubs matches King of Spades
---------- Game is Over
Hand Allen is empty

Hand Jeff contains
Queen of Spades

Hand Chris is empty
```

So Jeff loses.

16.8 Glossary

inheritance: The ability to define a new class that is a modified version of a previously defined class.

parent class: The class from which a child class inherits.

child class: A new class created by inheriting from an existing class; also called a "subclass."

```
Hand Allen picked King of Diamonds
Hand Allen: King of Hearts matches King of Diamonds
Hand Jeff picked 10 of Hearts
Hand Chris picked Jack of Clubs
Hand Allen picked Jack of Hearts
Hand Jeff picked Jack of Diamonds
Hand Chris picked Queen of Spades
Hand Allen picked Jack of Diamonds
Hand Allen: Jack of Hearts matches Jack of Diamonds
Hand Jeff picked King of Clubs
Hand Chris picked King of Spades
Hand Allen picked 10 of Hearts
Hand Allen: 10 of Diamonds matches 10 of Hearts
Hand Jeff picked Queen of Spades
Hand Chris picked Jack of Spades
Hand Chris: Jack of Clubs matches Jack of Spades
Hand Jeff picked King of Spades
Hand Jeff: King of Clubs matches King of Spades
---------- Game is Over
Hand Allen is empty

Hand Jeff contains
Queen of Spades

Hand Chris is empty
```

So Jeff loses.

16.8 Glossary

inheritance: The ability to define a new class that is a modified version of a previously defined class.

parent class: The class from which a child class inherits.

child class: A new class created by inheriting from an existing class; also called a "subclass."

Chapter 17

Linked lists

17.1 Embedded references

We have seen examples of attributes that refer to other objects, which we called **embedded references** (see Section 12.8). A common data structure, the **linked list**, takes advantage of this feature.

Linked lists are made up of **nodes**, where each node contains a reference to the next node in the list. In addition, each node contains a unit of data called the **cargo**.

A linked list is considered a **recursive data structure** because it has a recursive definition.

> A linked list is either:
>
> - the empty list, represented by `None`, or
> - a node that contains a cargo object and a reference to a linked list.

Recursive data structures lend themselves to recursive methods.

17.2 The `Node` class

As usual when writing a new class, we'll start with the initialization and `__str__` methods so that we can test the basic mechanism of creating and displaying the new type:

```
class Node:
  def __init__(self, cargo=None, next=None):
    self.cargo = cargo
    self.next  = next

  def __str__(self):
    return str(self.cargo)
```

As usual, the parameters for the initialization method are optional. By default, both the cargo and the link, **next**, are set to **None**.

The string representation of a node is just the string representation of the cargo. Since any value can be passed to the **str** function, we can store any value in a list.

To test the implementation so far, we can create a **Node** and print it:

```
>>> node = Node("test")
>>> print node
test
```

To make it interesting, we need a list with more than one node:

```
>>> node1 = Node(1)
>>> node2 = Node(2)
>>> node3 = Node(3)
```

This code creates three nodes, but we don't have a list yet because the nodes are not **linked**. The state diagram looks like this:

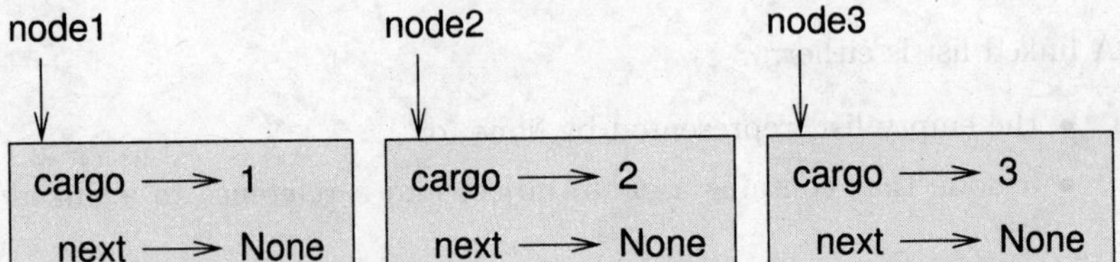

To link the nodes, we have to make the first node refer to the second and the second node refer to the third:

```
>>> node1.next = node2
>>> node2.next = node3
```

The reference of the third node is **None**, which indicates that it is the end of the list. Now the state diagram looks like this:

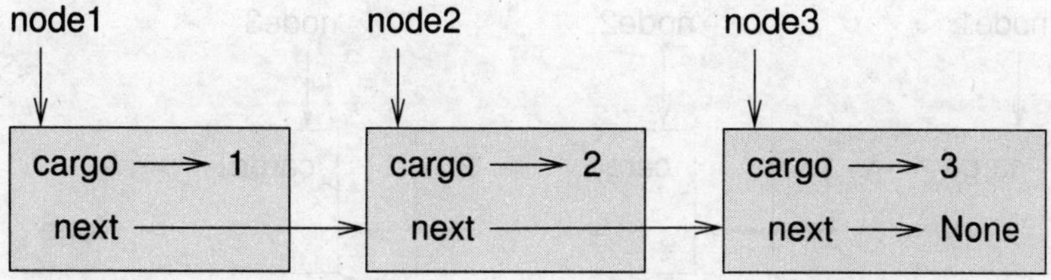

Now you know how to create nodes and link them into lists. What might be less clear at this point is why.

17.3 Lists as collections

Lists are useful because they provide a way to assemble multiple objects into a single entity, sometimes called a **collection**. In the example, the first node of the list serves as a reference to the entire list.

To pass the list as an argument, we only have to pass a reference to the first node. For example, the function `printList` takes a single node as an argument. Starting with the head of the list, it prints each node until it gets to the end:

```
def printList(node):
  while node:
    print node,
    node = node.next
  print
```

To invoke this function, we pass a reference to the first node:

```
>>> printList(node1)
1 2 3
```

Inside `printList` we have a reference to the first node of the list, but there is no variable that refers to the other nodes. We have to use the `next` value from each node to get to the next node.

To traverse a linked list, it is common to use a loop variable like `node` to refer to each of the nodes in succession.

This diagram shows the nodes in the list and the values that `node` takes on:

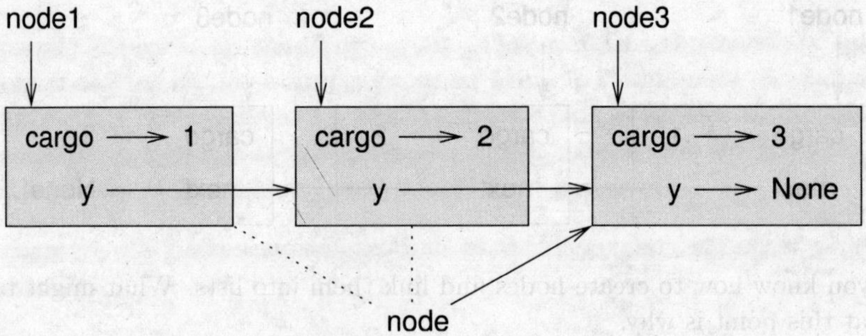

By convention, lists are often printed in brackets with commas between the elements, as in `[1, 2, 3]`*. As an exercise, modify* `printList` *so that it generates output in this format.*

17.4 Lists and recursion

It is natural to express many list operations using recursive methods. For example, the following is a recursive algorithm for printing a list backwards:

1. Separate the list into two pieces: the first node (called the head); and the rest (called the tail).
2. Print the tail backward.
3. Print the head.

Of course, Step 2, the recursive call, assumes that we have a way of printing a list backward. But if we assume that the recursive call works—the leap of faith—then we can convince ourselves that this algorithm works.

All we need are a base case and a way of proving that for any list, we will eventually get to the base case. Given the recursive definition of a list, a natural base case is the empty list, represented by `None`:

```
def printBackward(list):
  if list == None: return
  head = list
  tail = list.next
  printBackward(tail)
  print head,
```

The first line handles the base case by doing nothing. The next two lines split the list into `head` and `tail`. The last two lines print the list. The comma at the end of the last line keeps Python from printing a newline after each node.

We invoke this function as we invoked `printList`:

```
>>> printBackward(node1)
3 2 1
```

The result is a backward list.

You might wonder why `printList` and `printBackward` are functions and not methods in the `Node` class. The reason is that we want to use `None` to represent the empty list and it is not legal to invoke a method on `None`. This limitation makes it awkward to write list-manipulating code in a clean object-oriented style.

Can we prove that `printBackward` will always terminate? In other words, will it always reach the base case? In fact, the answer is no. Some lists will make this function crash.

17.5 Infinite lists

There is nothing to prevent a node from referring back to an earlier node in the list, including itself. For example, this figure shows a list with two nodes, one of which refers to itself:

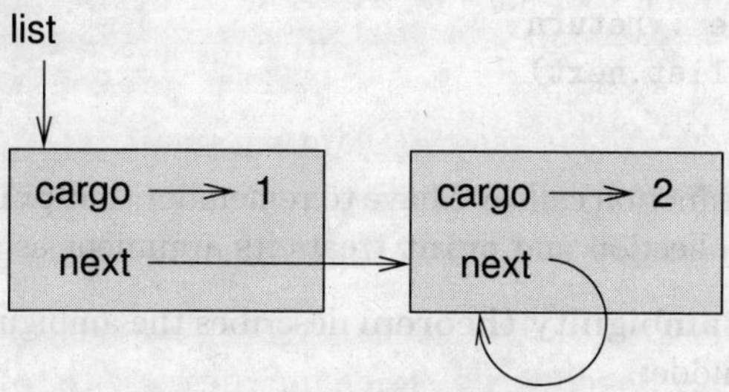

If we invoke `printList` on this list, it will loop forever. If we invoke `printBackward`, it will recurse infinitely. This sort of behavior makes infinite lists difficult to work with.

Nevertheless, they are occasionally useful. For example, we might represent a number as a list of digits and use an infinite list to represent a repeating fraction.

Regardless, it is problematic that we cannot prove that `printList` and `printBackward` terminate. The best we can do is the hypothetical statement, "If the list contains no loops, then these functions will terminate." This sort of claim is called a **precondition**. It imposes a constraint on one of the arguments and describes the behavior of the function if the constraint is satisfied. You will see more examples soon.

17.6 The fundamental ambiguity theorem

One part of `printBackward` might have raised an eyebrow:

```
head = list
tail = list.next
```

After the first assignment, `head` and `list` have the same type and the same value. So why did we create a new variable?

The reason is that the two variables play different roles. We think of `head` as a reference to a single node, and we think of `list` as a reference to the first node of a list. These "roles" are not part of the program; they are in the mind of the programmer.

In general we can't tell by looking at a program what role a variable plays. This ambiguity can be useful, but it can also make programs difficult to read. We often use variable names like `node` and `list` to document how we intend to use a variable and sometimes create additional variables to disambiguate.

We could have written `printBackward` without `head` and `tail`, which makes it more concise but possibly less clear:

```
def printBackward(list) :
  if list == None : return
  printBackward(list.next)
  print list,
```

Looking at the two function calls, we have to remember that `printBackward` treats its argument as a collection and `print` treats its argument as a single object.

The **fundamental ambiguity theorem** describes the ambiguity that is inherent in a reference to a node:

> **A variable that refers to a node might treat the node as a single object or as the first in a list of nodes.**

17.7 Modifying lists

There are two ways to modify a linked list. Obviously, we can change the cargo of one of the nodes, but the more interesting operations are the ones that add, remove, or reorder the nodes.

As an example, let's write a function that removes the second node in the list and returns a reference to the removed node:

```
def removeSecond(list):
  if list == None: return
  first = list
  second = list.next
  # make the first node refer to the third
  first.next = second.next
  # separate the second node from the rest of the list
  second.next = None
  return second
```

Again, we are using temporary variables to make the code more readable. Here is how to use this function:

```
>>> printList(node1)
1 2 3
>>> removed = removeSecond(node1)
>>> printList(removed)
2
>>> printList(node1)
1 3
```

This state diagram shows the effect of the operation:

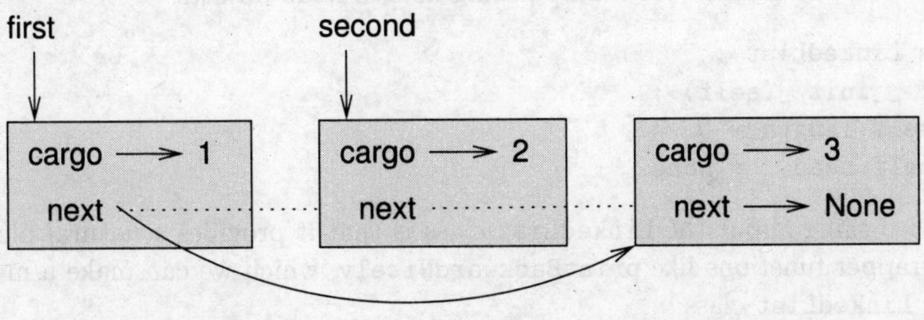

What happens if you invoke this function and pass a list with only one element (a **singleton**)? What happens if you pass the empty list as an argument? Is there a precondition for this function? If so, fix the function to handle a violation of the precondition in a reasonable way.

17.8 Wrappers and helpers

It is often useful to divide a list operation into two functions. For example, to print a list backward in the format `[3 2 1]` we can use the `printBackward` function to print `3 2 1` but we need a separate function to print the brackets. Let's call it `printBackwardNicely`:

```
def printBackwardNicely(list) :
  print "[",
  printBackward(list)
  print "]",
```

Again, it is a good idea to check functions like this to see if they work with special cases like an empty list or a singleton.

When we use this function elsewhere in the program, we invoke `printBackwardNicely` directly, and it invokes `printBackward` on our behalf. In that sense, `printBackwardNicely` acts as a **wrapper**, and it uses `printBackward` as a **helper**.

17.9 The LinkedList class

There are some subtle problems with the way we have been implementing lists. In a reversal of cause and effect, we'll propose an alternative implementation first and then explain what problems it solves.

First, we'll create a new class called `LinkedList`. Its attributes are an integer that contains the length of the list and a reference to the first node. `LinkedList` objects serve as handles for manipulating lists of `Node` objects:

```
class LinkedList :
  def __init__(self) :
    self.length = 0
    self.head   = None
```

One nice thing about the `LinkedList` class is that it provides a natural place to put wrapper functions like `printBackwardNicely`, which we can make a method of the `LinkedList` class:

```
class LinkedList:
  ...
  def printBackward(self):
    print "[",
    if self.head != None:
      self.head.printBackward()
    print "]",

class Node:
  ...
  def printBackward(self):
    if self.next != None:
```

```
        tail = self.next
        tail.printBackward()
      print self.cargo,
```

Just to make things confusing, we renamed `printBackwardNicely`. Now there are two methods named `printBackward`: one in the `Node` class (the helper); and one in the `LinkedList` class (the wrapper). When the wrapper invokes `self.head.printBackward`, it is invoking the helper, because `self.head` is a `Node` object.

Another benefit of the `LinkedList` class is that it makes it easier to add or remove the first element of a list. For example, `addFirst` is a method for `LinkedLists`; it takes an item of cargo as an argument and puts it at the beginning of the list:

```
class LinkedList:
  ...
  def addFirst(self, cargo):
    node = Node(cargo)
    node.next = self.head
    self.head = node
    self.length = self.length + 1
```

As usual, you should check code like this to see if it handles the special cases. For example, what happens if the list is initially empty?

17.10 Invariants

Some lists are "well formed"; others are not. For example, if a list contains a loop, it will cause many of our methods to crash, so we might want to require that lists contain no loops. Another requirement is that the `length` value in the `LinkedList` object should be equal to the actual number of nodes in the list.

Requirements like these are called **invariants** because, ideally, they should be true of every object all the time. Specifying invariants for objects is a useful programming practice because it makes it easier to prove the correctness of code, check the integrity of data structures, and detect errors.

One thing that is sometimes confusing about invariants is that there are times when they are violated. For example, in the middle of `addFirst`, after we have added the node but before we have incremented `length`, the invariant is violated. This kind of violation is acceptable; in fact, it is often impossible to modify an object without violating an invariant for at least a little while. Normally, we require that every method that violates an invariant must restore the invariant.

If there is any significant stretch of code in which the invariant is violated, it is important for the comments to make that clear, so that no operations are performed that depend on the invariant.

17.11 Glossary

embedded reference: A reference stored in an attribute of an object.

linked list: A data structure that implements a collection using a sequence of linked nodes.

node: An element of a list, usually implemented as an object that contains a reference to another object of the same type.

cargo: An item of data contained in a node.

link: An embedded reference used to link one object to another.

precondition: An assertion that must be true in order for a method to work correctly.

fundamental ambiguity theorem: A reference to a list node can be treated as a single object or as the first in a list of nodes.

singleton: A linked list with a single node.

wrapper: A method that acts as a middleman between a caller and a helper method, often making the method easier or less error-prone to invoke.

helper: A method that is not invoked directly by a caller but is used by another method to perform part of an operation.

invariant: An assertion that should be true of an object at all times (except perhaps while the object is being modified).

Chapter 18

Stacks

18.1 Abstract data types

The data types you have seen so far are all concrete, in the sense that we have completely specified how they are implemented. For example, the `Card` class represents a card using two integers. As we discussed at the time, that is not the only way to represent a card; there are many alternative implementations.

An **abstract data type**, or ADT, specifies a set of operations (or methods) and the semantics of the operations (what they do), but it does not specify the implementation of the operations. That's what makes it abstract.

Why is that useful?

- It simplifies the task of specifying an algorithm if you can denote the operations you need without having to think at the same time about how the operations are performed.
- Since there are usually many ways to implement an ADT, it might be useful to write an algorithm that can be used with any of the possible implementations.
- Well-known ADTs, such as the Stack ADT in this chapter, are often implemented in standard libraries so they can be written once and used by many programmers.
- The operations on ADTs provide a common high-level language for specifying and talking about algorithms.

When we talk about ADTs, we often distinguish the code that uses the ADT, called the **client** code, from the code that implements the ADT, called the **provider** code.

18.2 The Stack ADT

In this chapter, we will look at one common ADT, the **stack**. A stack is a collection, meaning that it is a data structure that contains multiple elements. Other collections we have seen include dictionaries and lists.

An ADT is defined by the operations that can be performed on it, which is called an **interface**. The interface for a stack consists of these operations:

`__init__`: Initialize a new empty stack.

`push`: Add a new item to the stack.

`pop`: Remove and return an item from the stack. The item that is returned is always the last one that was added.

`isEmpty`: Check whether the stack is empty.

A stack is sometimes called a "last in, first out" or LIFO data structure, because the last item added is the first to be removed.

18.3 Implementing stacks with Python lists

The list operations that Python provides are similar to the operations that define a stack. The interface isn't exactly what it is supposed to be, but we can write code to translate from the Stack ADT to the built-in operations.

This code is called an **implementation** of the Stack ADT. In general, an implementation is a set of methods that satisfy the syntactic and semantic requirements of an interface.

Here is an implementation of the Stack ADT that uses a Python list:

```
class Stack :
  def __init__(self) :
    self.items = []

  def push(self, item) :
    self.items.append(item)
```

```
  def pop(self) :
    return self.items.pop()

  def isEmpty(self) :
    return (self.items == [])
```

A `Stack` object contains an attribute named `items` that is a list of items in the stack. The initialization method sets `items` to the empty list.

To push a new item onto the stack, `push` appends it onto `items`. To pop an item off the stack, `pop` uses the homonymous[1] list method to remove and return the last item on the list.

Finally, to check if the stack is empty, `isEmpty` compares `items` to the empty list.

An implementation like this, in which the methods consist of simple invocations of existing methods, is called a **veneer**. In real life, veneer is a thin coating of good quality wood used in furniture-making to hide lower quality wood underneath. Computer scientists use this metaphor to describe a small piece of code that hides the details of an implementation and provides a simpler, or more standard, interface.

18.4 Pushing and popping

A stack is a **generic data structure**, which means that we can add any type of item to it. The following example pushes two integers and a string onto the stack:

```
>>> s = Stack()
>>> s.push(54)
>>> s.push(45)
>>> s.push("+")
```

We can use `isEmpty` and `pop` to remove and print all of the items on the stack:

```
while not s.isEmpty() :
  print s.pop(),
```

The output is `+ 45 54`. In other words, we just used a stack to print the items backward! Granted, it's not the standard format for printing a list, but by using a stack, it was remarkably easy to do.

You should compare this bit of code to the implementation of `printBackward` in Section 17.4. There is a natural parallel between the recursive version

[1] same-named

of `printBackward` and the stack algorithm here. The difference is that `printBackward` uses the runtime stack to keep track of the nodes while it traverses the list, and then prints them on the way back from the recursion. The stack algorithm does the same thing, except that it uses a `Stack` object instead of the runtime stack.

18.5 Using a stack to evaluate postfix

In most programming languages, mathematical expressions are written with the operator between the two operands, as in `1+2`. This format is called **infix**. An alternative used by some calculators is called **postfix**. In postfix, the operator follows the operands, as in `1 2 +`.

The reason postfix is sometimes useful is that there is a natural way to evaluate a postfix expression using a stack:

- Starting at the beginning of the expression, get one term (operator or operand) at a time.
  - If the term is an operand, push it on the stack.
  - If the term is an operator, pop two operands off the stack, perform the operation on them, and push the result back on the stack.
- When you get to the end of the expression, there should be exactly one operand left on the stack. That operand is the result.

As an exercise, apply this algorithm to the expression `1 2 + 3 *`.

This example demonstrates one of the advantages of postfix—there is no need to use parentheses to control the order of operations. To get the same result in infix, we would have to write `(1 + 2) * 3`.

As an exercise, write a postfix expression that is equivalent to `1 + 2 * 3`.

18.6 Parsing

To implement the previous algorithm, we need to be able to traverse a string and break it into operands and operators. This process is an example of **parsing**, and the results—the individual chunks of the string—are called **tokens**. You might remember these words from Chapter 1.

Python provides a split method in both the string and re (regular expression) modules. The function string.split splits a string into a list using a single character as a **delimiter**. For example:

```
>>> import string
>>> string.split("Now is the time"," ")
['Now', 'is', 'the', 'time']
```

In this case, the delimiter is the space character, so the string is split at each space.

The function re.split is more powerful, allowing us to provide a regular expression instead of a delimiter. A regular expression is a way of specifying a set of strings. For example, [A-z] is the set of all letters and [0-9] is the set of all digits. The ^ operator negates a set, so [^0-9] is the set of every character that is not a digit, which is exactly the set we want to use to split up postfix expressions:

```
>>> import re
>>> re.split("([^0-9])", "123+456*/")
['123', '+', '456', '*', '', '/', '']
```

Notice that the order of the arguments is different from string.split; the delimiter comes before the string.

The resulting list includes the operands 123 and 456 and the operators * and /. It also includes two empty strings that are inserted as "phantom operands," whenever an operator appears without a number before or after it.

18.7 Evaluating postfix

To evaluate a postfix expression, we will use the parser from the previous section and the algorithm from the section before that. To keep things simple, we'll start with an evaluator that only implements the operators + and *:

```
def evalPostfix(expr):
  import re
  tokenList = re.split("([^0-9])", expr)
  stack = Stack()
  for token in tokenList:
    if  token == '' or token == ' ':
      continue
    if  token == '+':
      sum = stack.pop() + stack.pop()
      stack.push(sum)
    elif token == '*':
      product = stack.pop() * stack.pop()
      stack.push(product)
    else:
      stack.push(int(token))
  return stack.pop()
```

The first condition takes care of spaces and empty strings. The next two conditions handle operators. We assume, for now, that anything else must be an operand. Of course, it would be better to check for erroneous input and report an error message, but we'll get to that later.

Let's test it by evaluating the postfix form of `(56+47)*2`:

```
>>> print evalPostfix ("56 47 + 2 *")
206
```

That's close enough.

18.8 Clients and providers

One of the fundamental goals of an ADT is to separate the interests of the provider, who writes the code that implements the ADT, and the client, who uses the ADT. The provider only has to worry about whether the implementation is correct—in accord with the specification of the ADT—and not how it will be used.

Conversely, the client *assumes* that the implementation of the ADT is correct and doesn't worry about the details. When you are using one of Python's built-in types, you have the luxury of thinking exclusively as a client.

Of course, when you implement an ADT, you also have to write client code to test it. In that case, you play both roles, which can be confusing. You should make some effort to keep track of which role you are playing at any moment.

18.9 Glossary

abstract data type (ADT): A data type (usually a collection of objects) that is defined by a set of operations but that can be implemented in a variety of ways.

interface: The set of operations that define an ADT.

implementation: Code that satisfies the syntactic and semantic requirements of an interface.

client: A program (or the person who wrote it) that uses an ADT.

provider: The code (or the person who wrote it) that implements an ADT.

veneer: A class definition that implements an ADT with method definitions that are invocations of other methods, sometimes with simple transformations. The veneer does no significant work, but it improves or standardizes the interface seen by the client.

generic data structure: A kind of data structure that can contain data of any type.

infix: A way of writing mathematical expressions with the operators between the operands.

postfix: A way of writing mathematical expressions with the operators after the operands.

parse: To read a string of characters or tokens and analyze its grammatical structure.

token: A set of characters that are treated as a unit for purposes of parsing, such as the words in a natural language.

delimiter: A character that is used to separate tokens, such as punctuation in a natural language.

Chapter 19

Queues

This chapter presents two ADTs: the Queue and the Priority Queue. In real life, a **queue** is a line of customers waiting for service of some kind. In most cases, the first customer in line is the next customer to be served. There are exceptions, though. At airports, customers whose flights are leaving soon are sometimes taken from the middle of the queue. At supermarkets, a polite customer might let someone with only a few items go first.

The rule that determines who goes next is called the **queueing policy**. The simplest queueing policy is called **FIFO**, for "first-in-first-out." The most general queueing policy is **priority queueing**, in which each customer is assigned a priority and the customer with the highest priority goes first, regardless of the order of arrival. We say this is the most general policy because the priority can be based on anything: what time a flight leaves; how many groceries the customer has; or how important the customer is. Of course, not all queueing policies are "fair," but fairness is in the eye of the beholder.

The Queue ADT and the Priority Queue ADT have the same set of operations. The difference is in the semantics of the operations: a queue uses the FIFO policy; and a priority queue (as the name suggests) uses the priority queueing policy.

19.1 The Queue ADT

The Queue ADT is defined by the following operations:

`__init__`: Initialize a new empty queue.

`insert`: Add a new item to the queue.

`remove`: Remove and return an item from the queue. The item that is returned is the first one that was added.

`isEmpty`: Check whether the queue is empty.

19.2 Linked Queue

The first implementation of the Queue ADT we will look at is called a **linked queue** because it is made up of linked `Node` objects. Here is the class definition:

```
class Queue:
  def __init__(self):
    self.length = 0
    self.head = None

  def isEmpty(self):
    return (self.length == 0)

  def insert(self, cargo):
    node = Node(cargo)
    node.next = None
    if self.head == None:
      # if list is empty the new node goes first
      self.head = node
    else:
      # find the last node in the list
      last = self.head
      while last.next: last = last.next
      # append the new node
      last.next = node
    self.length = self.length + 1

  def remove(self):
    cargo = self.head.cargo
    self.head = self.head.next
    self.length = self.length - 1
    return cargo
```

The methods `isEmpty` and `remove` are identical to the `LinkedList` methods `isEmpty` and `removeFirst`. The `insert` method is new and a bit more complicated.

We want to insert new items at the end of the list. If the queue is empty, we just set `head` to refer to the new node.

Otherwise, we traverse the list to the last node and tack the new node on the end. We can identify the last node because its `next` attribute is `None`.

There are two invariants for a properly formed `Queue` object. The value of `length` should be the number of nodes in the queue, and the last node should have `next` equal to `None`. Convince yourself that this method preserves both invariants.

19.3 Performance characteristics

Normally when we invoke a method, we are not concerned with the details of its implementation. But there is one "detail" we might want to know—the performance characteristics of the method. How long does it take, and how does the run time change as the number of items in the collection increases?

First look at `remove`. There are no loops or function calls here, suggesting that the runtime of this method is the same every time. Such a method is called a **constant time** operation. In reality, the method might be slightly faster when the list is empty since it skips the body of the conditional, but that difference is not significant.

The performance of `insert` is very different. In the general case, we have to traverse the list to find the last element.

This traversal takes time proportional to the length of the list. Since the runtime is a linear function of the length, this method is called **linear time**. Compared to constant time, that's very bad.

19.4 Improved Linked Queue

We would like an implementation of the Queue ADT that can perform all operations in constant time. One way to do that is to modify the Queue class so that it maintains a reference to both the first and the last node, as shown in the figure:

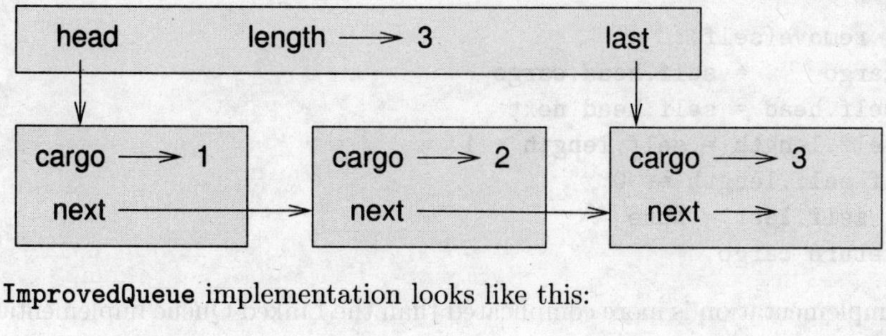

The `ImprovedQueue` implementation looks like this:

```
class ImprovedQueue:
  def __init__(self):
    self.length = 0
    self.head   = None
    self.last   = None

  def isEmpty(self):
    return (self.length == 0)
```

So far, the only change is the attribute `last`. It is used in `insert` and `remove` methods:

```
class ImprovedQueue:
  ...
  def insert(self, cargo):
    node = Node(cargo)
    node.next = None
    if self.length == 0:
      # if list is empty, the new node is head and last
      self.head = self.last = node
    else:
      # find the last node
      last = self.last
      # append the new node
      last.next = node
      self.last = node
    self.length = self.length + 1
```

Since `last` keeps track of the last node, we don't have to search for it. As a result, this method is constant time.

There is a price to pay for that speed. We have to add a special case to `remove` to set `last` to `None` when the last node is removed:

```
class ImprovedQueue:
  ...
  def remove(self):
    cargo      = self.head.cargo
    self.head = self.head.next
    self.length = self.length - 1
    if self.length == 0:
      self.last = None
    return cargo
```

This implementation is more complicated than the Linked Queue implementation, and it is more difficult to demonstrate that it is correct. The advantage is that we have achieved the goal—both `insert` and `remove` are constant time operations.

> *As an exercise, write an implementation of the Queue ADT using a Python list. Compare the performance of this implementation to the* `ImprovedQueue` *for a range of queue lengths.*

19.5 Priority queue

The Priority Queue ADT has the same interface as the Queue ADT, but different semantics. Again, the interface is:

`__init__`: Initialize a new empty queue.

`insert`: Add a new item to the queue.

`remove`: Remove and return an item from the queue. The item that is returned is the one with the highest priority.

`isEmpty`: Check whether the queue is empty.

The semantic difference is that the item that is removed from the queue is not necessarily the first one that was added. Rather, it is the item in the queue that has the highest priority. What the priorities are and how they compare to each other are not specified by the Priority Queue implementation. It depends on which items are in the queue.

For example, if the items in the queue have names, we might choose them in alphabetical order. If they are bowling scores, we might go from highest to lowest, but if they are golf scores, we would go from lowest to highest. As long as we can compare the items in the queue, we can find and remove the one with the highest priority.

This implementation of Priority Queue has as an attribute a Python list that contains the items in the queue.

```
class PriorityQueue:
  def __init__(self):
    self.items = []

  def isEmpty(self):
    return self.items == []

  def insert(self, item):
    self.items.append(item)
```

The initialization method, isEmpty, and insert are all veneers on list operations. The only interesting method is remove:

```
class PriorityQueue:
  ...
  def remove(self):
    maxi = 0
    for i in range(1,len(self.items)):
      if self.items[i] > self.items[maxi]:
        maxi = i
    item = self.items[maxi]
    self.items[maxi:maxi+1] = []
    return item
```

At the beginning of each iteration, maxi holds the index of the biggest item (highest priority) we have seen *so far*. Each time through the loop, the program compares the i-eth item to the champion. If the new item is bigger, the value of maxi is set to i.

When the for statement completes, maxi is the index of the biggest item. This item is removed from the list and returned.

Let's test the implementation:

```
>>> q = PriorityQueue()
>>> q.insert(11)
>>> q.insert(12)
>>> q.insert(14)
>>> q.insert(13)
>>> while not q.isEmpty(): print q.remove()
14
13
12
11
```

If the queue contains simple numbers or strings, they are removed in numerical or alphabetical order, from highest to lowest. Python can find the biggest integer or string because it can compare them using the built-in comparison operators.

If the queue contains an object type, it has to provide a __cmp__ method. When remove uses the > operator to compare items, it invokes the __cmp__ for one of the items and passes the other as an argument. As long as the __cmp__ method works correctly, the Priority Queue will work.

19.6 The Golfer class

As an example of an object with an unusual definition of priority, let's implement a class called `Golfer` that keeps track of the names and scores of golfers. As usual, we start by defining `__init__` and `__str__`:

```
class Golfer:
  def __init__(self, name, score):
    self.name = name
    self.score= score

  def __str__(self):
    return "%-16s: %d" % (self.name, self.score)
```

`__str__` uses the format operator to put the names and scores in neat columns.

Next we define a version of `__cmp__` where the lowest score gets highest priority. As always, `__cmp__` returns 1 if `self` is "greater than" `other`, -1 if `self` is "less than" other, and 0 if they are equal.

```
class Golfer:
  ...
  def __cmp__(self, other):
    if self.score < other.score: return  1   # less is more
    if self.score > other.score: return -1
    return 0
```

Now we are ready to test the priority queue with the `Golfer` class:

```
>>> tiger = Golfer("Tiger Woods",    61)
>>> phil  = Golfer("Phil Mickelson", 72)
>>> hal   = Golfer("Hal Sutton",     69)
>>>
>>> pq = PriorityQueue()
>>> pq.insert(tiger)
>>> pq.insert(phil)
>>> pq.insert(hal)
>>> while not pq.isEmpty(): print pq.remove()
Tiger Woods    : 61
Hal Sutton     : 69
Phil Mickelson : 72
```

As an exercise, write an implementation of the Priority Queue ADT using a linked list. You should keep the list sorted so that removal is a constant time operation. Compare the performance of this implementation with the Python list implementation.

19.7 Glossary

queue: An ordered set of objects waiting for a service of some kind.

Queue: An ADT that performs the operations one might perform on a queue.

queueing policy: The rules that determine which member of a queue is removed next.

FIFO: "First In, First Out," a queueing policy in which the first member to arrive is the first to be removed.

priority queue: A queueing policy in which each member has a priority determined by external factors. The member with the highest priority is the first to be removed.

Priority Queue: An ADT that defines the operations one might perform on a priority queue.

linked queue: An implementation of a queue using a linked list.

constant time: An operation whose runtime does not depend on the size of the data structure.

linear time: An operation whose runtime is a linear function of the size of the data structure.

Chapter 20

Trees

Like linked lists, trees are made up of nodes. A common kind of tree is a **binary tree**, in which each node contains a reference to two other nodes (possibly null). These references are referred to as the left and right subtrees. Like list nodes, tree nodes also contain cargo. A state diagram for a tree looks like this:

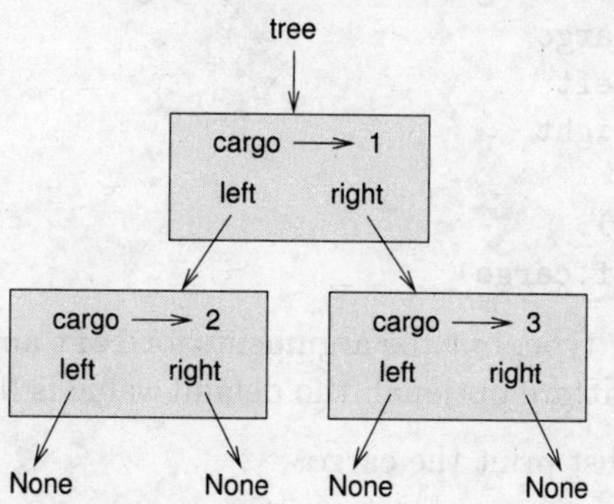

To avoid cluttering up the picture, we often omit the `None`s.

The top of the tree (the node `tree` refers to) is called the **root**. In keeping with the tree metaphor, the other nodes are called branches and the nodes at the tips with null references are called **leaves**. It may seem odd that we draw the picture with the root at the top and the leaves at the bottom, but that is not the strangest thing.

To make things worse, computer scientists mix in another metaphor—the family tree. The top node is sometimes called a **parent** and the nodes it refers to are its **children**. Nodes with the same parent are called **siblings**.

Finally, there is a geometric vocabulary for talking about trees. We already mentioned left and right, but there is also "up" (toward the parent/root) and "down" (toward the children/leaves). Also, all of the nodes that are the same distance from the root comprise a **level** of the tree.

We probably don't need three metaphors for talking about trees, but there they are.

Like linked lists, trees are recursive data structures because they are defined recursively.

> A tree is either:
>
> - the empty tree, represented by `None`, or
> - a node that contains an object reference and two tree references.

20.1 Building trees

The process of assembling a tree is similar to the process of assembling a linked list. Each constructor invocation builds a single node.

```
class Tree:
  def __init__(self, cargo, left=None, right=None):
    self.cargo = cargo
    self.left  = left
    self.right = right

  def __str__(self):
    return str(self.cargo)
```

The `cargo` can be any type, but the arguments for `left` and `right` should be tree nodes. `left` and `right` are optional; the default value is `None`.

To print a node, we just print the cargo.

One way to build a tree is from the bottom up. Allocate the child nodes first:

```
left = Tree(2)
right = Tree(3)
```

Then create the parent node and link it to the children:

```
tree = Tree(1, left, right);
```

We can write this code more concisely by nesting constructor invocations:

```
>>> tree = Tree(1, Tree(2), Tree(3))
```

Either way, the result is the tree at the beginning of the chapter.

20.2 Traversing trees

Any time you see a new data structure, your first question should be, "How do I traverse it?" The most natural way to traverse a tree is recursively. For example, if the tree contains integers as cargo, this function returns their sum:

```
def total(tree):
  if tree == None: return 0
  return total(tree.left) + total(tree.right) + tree.cargo
```

The base case is the empty tree, which contains no cargo, so the sum is 0. The recursive step makes two recursive calls to find the sum of the child trees. When the recursive calls complete, we add the cargo of the parent and return the total.

20.3 Expression trees

A tree is a natural way to represent the structure of an expression. Unlike other notations, it can represent the computation unambiguously. For example, the infix expression `1 + 2 * 3` is ambiguous unless we know that the multiplication happens before the addition.

This expression tree represents the same computation:

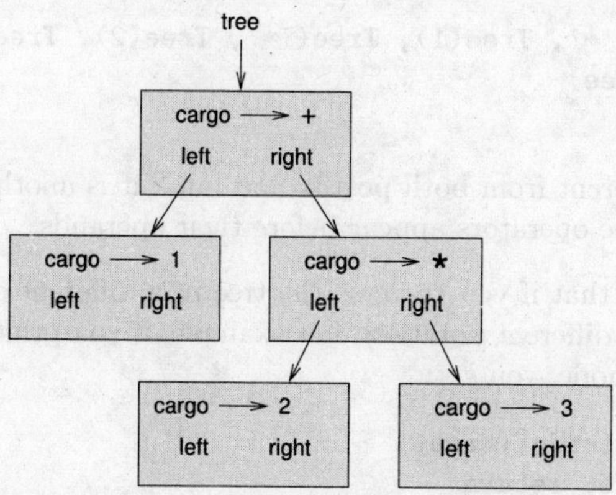

The nodes of an expression tree can be operands like `1` and `2` or operators like `+` and `*`. Operands are leaf nodes; operator nodes contain references to their operands. (All of these operators are **binary**, meaning they have exactly two operands.)

We can build this tree like this:

```
>>> tree = Tree('+', Tree(1), Tree('*', Tree(2), Tree(3)))
```

Looking at the figure, there is no question what the order of operations is; the multiplication happens first in order to compute the second operand of the addition.

Expression trees have many uses. The example in this chapter uses trees to translate expressions to postfix, prefix, and infix. Similar trees are used inside compilers to parse, optimize, and translate programs.

20.4 Tree traversal

We can traverse an expression tree and print the contents like this:

```
def printTree(tree):
  if tree == None: return
  print tree.cargo,
  printTree(tree.left)
  printTree(tree.right)
```

In other words, to print a tree, first print the contents of the root, then print the entire left subtree, and then print the entire right subtree. This way of traversing a tree is called a **preorder**, because the contents of the root appear *before* the contents of the children. For the previous example, the output is:

```
>>> tree = Tree('+', Tree(1), Tree('*', Tree(2), Tree(3)))
>>> printTree(tree)
+ 1 * 2 3
```

This format is different from both postfix and infix; it is another notation called **prefix**, in which the operators appear before their operands.

You might suspect that if you traverse the tree in a different order, you will get the expression in a different notation. For example, if you print the subtrees first and then the root node, you get:

```
def printTreePostorder(tree):
  if tree == None: return
  printTreePostorder(tree.left)
  printTreePostorder(tree.right)
  print tree.cargo,
```

The result, `1 2 3 * +`, is in postfix! This order of traversal is called **postorder**.

Finally, to traverse a tree **inorder**, you print the left tree, then the root, and then the right tree:

```
def printTreeInorder(tree):
  if tree == None: return
  printTreeInorder(tree.left)
  print tree.cargo,
  printTreeInorder(tree.right)
```

The result is `1 + 2 * 3`, which is the expression in infix.

To be fair, we should point out that we have omitted an important complication. Sometimes when we write an expression in infix, we have to use parentheses to preserve the order of operations. So an inorder traversal is not quite sufficient to generate an infix expression.

Nevertheless, with a few improvements, the expression tree and the three recursive traversals provide a general way to translate expressions from one format to another.

> *As an exercise, modify* `printTreeInorder` *so that it puts parentheses around every operator and pair of operands. Is the output correct and unambiguous? Are the parentheses always necessary?*

If we do an inorder traversal and keep track of what level in the tree we are on, we can generate a graphical representation of a tree:

```
def printTreeIndented(tree, level=0):
  if tree == None: return
  printTreeIndented(tree.right, level+1)
  print '  '*level + str(tree.cargo)
  printTreeIndented(tree.left, level+1)
```

The parameter `level` keeps track of where we are in the tree. By default, it is initially 0. Each time we make a recursive call, we pass `level+1` because the child's level is always one greater than the parent's. Each item is indented by two spaces per level. The result for the example tree is:

```
>>> printTreeIndented(tree)
    3
  *
    2
+
  1
```

If you look at the output sideways, you see a simplified version of the original figure.

20.5 Building an expression tree

In this section, we parse infix expressions and build the corresponding expression trees. For example, the expression (3+7)*9 yields the following tree:

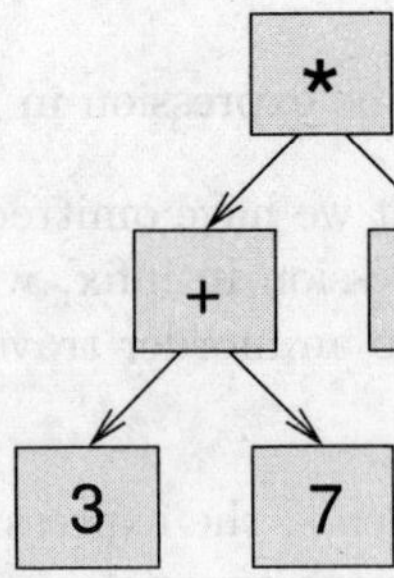

Notice that we have simplified the diagram by leaving out the names of the attributes.

The parser we will write handles expressions that include numbers, parentheses, and the operators + and *. We assume that the input string has already been tokenized into a Python list. The token list for (3+7)*9 is:

```
['(', 3, '+', 7, ')', '*', 9, 'end']
```

The end token is useful for preventing the parser from reading past the end of the list.

> *As an exercise, write a function that takes an expression string and returns a token list.*

The first function we'll write is getToken, which takes a token list and an expected token as arguments. It compares the expected token to the first token on the list: if they match, it removes the token from the list and returns true; otherwise, it returns false:

```
def getToken(tokenList, expected):
  if tokenList[0] == expected:
    del tokenList[0]
    return True
  else:
    return False
```

Since tokenList refers to a mutable object, the changes made here are visible to any other variable that refers to the same object.

The next function, getNumber, handles operands. If the next token in tokenList is a number, getNumber removes it and returns a leaf node containing the number; otherwise, it returns None.

```
def getNumber(tokenList):
  x = tokenList[0]
  if not isinstance(x, int): return None
  del tokenList[0]
  return Tree (x, None, None)
```

Before continuing, we should test getNumber in isolation. We assign a list of numbers to tokenList, extract the first, print the result, and print what remains of the token list:

```
>>> tokenList = [9, 11, 'end']
>>> x = getNumber(tokenList)
>>> printTreePostorder(x)
9
>>> print tokenList
[11, 'end']
```

The next method we need is getProduct, which builds an expression tree for products. A simple product has two numbers as operands, like 3 * 7.

Here is a version of getProduct that handles simple products.

```
def getProduct(tokenList):
  a = getNumber(tokenList)
  if getToken(tokenList, '*'):
    b = getNumber(tokenList)
    return Tree ('*', a, b)
  else:
    return a
```

Assuming that getNumber succeeds and returns a singleton tree, we assign the first operand to a. If the next character is *, we get the second number and build an expression tree with a, b, and the operator.

If the next character is anything else, then we just return the leaf node with a. Here are two examples:

```
>>> tokenList = [9, '*', 11, 'end']
>>> tree = getProduct(tokenList)
>>> printTreePostorder(tree)
9 11 *
```

```
>>> tokenList = [9, '+', 11, 'end']
>>> tree = getProduct(tokenList)
>>> printTreePostorder(tree)
9
```

The second example implies that we consider a single operand to be a kind of product. This definition of "product" is counterintuitive, but it turns out to be useful.

Now we have to deal with compound products, like like `3 * 5 * 13`. We treat this expression as a product of products, namely `3 * (5 * 13)`. The resulting tree is:

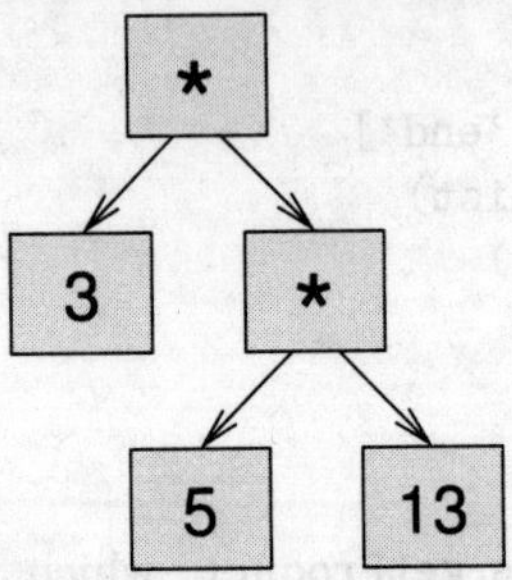

With a small change in `getProduct`, we can handle an arbitrarily long product:

```
def getProduct(tokenList):
  a = getNumber(tokenList)
  if getToken(tokenList, '*'):
    b = getProduct(tokenList)          # this line changed
    return Tree ('*', a, b)
  else:
    return a
```

In other words, a product can be either a singleton or a tree with `*` at the root, a number on the left, and a product on the right. This kind of recursive definition should be starting to feel familiar.

Let's test the new version with a compound product:

```
>>> tokenList = [2, '*', 3, '*', 5 , '*', 7, 'end']
>>> tree = getProduct(tokenList)
>>> printTreePostorder(tree)
2 3 5 7 * * *
```

Next we will add the ability to parse sums. Again, we use a slightly counterintuitive definition of "sum." For us, a sum can be a tree with `+` at the root, a product on the left, and a sum on the right. Or, a sum can be just a product.

If you are willing to play along with this definition, it has a nice property: we can represent any expression (without parentheses) as a sum of products. This property is the basis of our parsing algorithm.

getSum tries to build a tree with a product on the left and a sum on the right. But if it doesn't find a +, it just builds a product.

```
def getSum(tokenList):
  a = getProduct(tokenList)
  if getToken(tokenList, '+'):
    b = getSum(tokenList)
    return Tree ('+', a, b)
  else:
    return a
```

Let's test it with 9 * 11 + 5 * 7:

```
>>> tokenList = [9, '*', 11, '+', 5, '*', 7, 'end']
>>> tree = getSum(tokenList)
>>> printTreePostorder(tree)
9 11 * 5 7 * +
```

We are almost done, but we still have to handle parentheses. Anywhere in an expression where there can be a number, there can also be an entire sum enclosed in parentheses. We just need to modify getNumber to handle **subexpressions**:

```
def getNumber(tokenList):
  if getToken(tokenList, '('):
    x = getSum(tokenList)          # get the subexpression
    getToken(tokenList, ')')       # remove the closing parenthesis
    return x
  else:
    x = tokenList[0]
    if not isinstance(x, int): return None
    tokenList[0:1] = []
    return Tree (x, None, None)
```

Let's test this code with 9 * (11 + 5) * 7:

```
>>> tokenList = [9, '*', '(', 11, '+', 5, ')', '*', 7, 'end']
>>> tree = getSum(tokenList)
>>> printTreePostorder(tree)
9 11 5 + 7 * *
```

The parser handled the parentheses correctly; the addition happens before the multiplication.

In the final version of the program, it would be a good idea to give `getNumber` a name more descriptive of its new role.

20.6 Handling errors

Throughout the parser, we've been assuming that expressions are well-formed. For example, when we reach the end of a subexpression, we assume that the next character is a close parenthesis. If there is an error and the next character is something else, we should deal with it.

```
def getNumber(tokenList):
  if getToken(tokenList, '('):
    x = getSum(tokenList)
    if not getToken(tokenList, ')'):
      raise ValueError, 'missing parenthesis'
    return x
  else:
    # the rest of the function omitted
```

The `raise` statement creates an exception; in this case a `ValueError`. If the function that called `getNumber`, or one of the other functions in the traceback, handles the exception, then the program can continue. Otherwise, Python will print an error message and quit.

> *As an exercise, find other places in these functions where errors can occur and add appropriate* `raise` *statements. Test your code with improperly formed expressions.*

20.7 The animal tree

In this section, we develop a small program that uses a tree to represent a knowledge base.

The program interacts with the user to create a tree of questions and animal names. Here is a sample run:

```
Are you thinking of an animal? y
Is it a bird? n
What is the animals name? dog
What question would distinguish a dog from a bird? Can it fly
If the animal were dog the answer would be? n

Are you thinking of an animal? y
Can it fly? n
Is it a dog? n
What is the animals name? cat
What question would distinguish a cat from a dog? Does it bark
If the animal were cat the answer would be? n

Are you thinking of an animal? y
Can it fly? n
Does it bark? y
Is it a dog? y
I rule!

Are you thinking of an animal? n
```

Here is the tree this dialog builds:

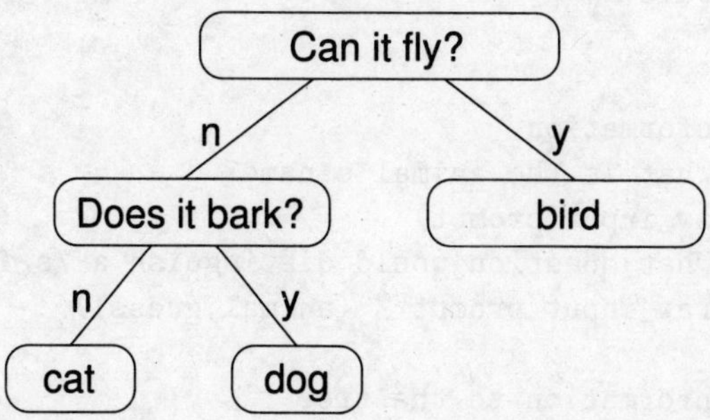

At the beginning of each round, the program starts at the top of the tree and asks the first question. Depending on the answer, it moves to the left or right child and continues until it gets to a leaf node. At that point, it makes a guess. If the guess is not correct, it asks the user for the name of the new animal and a question that distinguishes the (bad) guess from the new animal. Then it adds a node to the tree with the new question and the new animal.

Here is the code:

```
def animal():
  # start with a singleton
  root = Tree("bird")

  # loop until the user quits
  while True:
    print
    if not yes("Are you thinking of an animal? "): break

    # walk the tree
    tree = root
    while tree.getLeft() != None:
      prompt = tree.getCargo() + "? "
      if yes(prompt):
        tree = tree.getRight()
      else:
        tree = tree.getLeft()

    # make a guess
    guess = tree.getCargo()
    prompt = "Is it a " + guess + "? "
    if yes(prompt):
      print "I rule!"
      continue

    # get new information
    prompt   = "What is the animal's name? "
    animal   = raw_input(prompt)
    prompt   = "What question would distinguish a %s from a %s? "
    question = raw_input(prompt % (animal,guess))

    # add new information to the tree
    tree.setCargo(question)
    prompt = "If the animal were %s the answer would be? "
    if yes(prompt % animal):
      tree.setLeft(Tree(guess))
      tree.setRight(Tree(animal))
    else:
      tree.setLeft(Tree(animal))
      tree.setRight(Tree(guess))
```

The function yes is a helper; it prints a prompt and then takes input from the user. If the response begins with *y* or *Y*, the function returns true:

```
def yes(ques):
  from string import lower
  ans = lower(raw_input(ques))
  return (ans[0] == 'y')
```

The condition of the outer loop is `True`, which means it will continue until the `break` statement executes, if the user is not thinking of an animal.

The inner `while` loop walks the tree from top to bottom, guided by the user's responses.

When a new node is added to the tree, the new question replaces the cargo, and the two children are the new animal and the original cargo.

One shortcoming of the program is that when it exits, it forgets everything you carefully taught it!

> *As an exercise, think of various ways you might save the knowledge tree in a file. Implement the one you think is easiest.*

20.8 Glossary

binary tree: A tree in which each node refers to zero, one, or two dependent nodes.

root: The topmost node in a tree, with no parent.

leaf: A bottom-most node in a tree, with no children.

parent: The node that refers to a given node.

child: One of the nodes referred to by a node.

siblings: Nodes that share a common parent.

level: The set of nodes equidistant from the root.

binary operator: An operator that takes two operands.

subexpression: An expression in parentheses that acts as a single operand in a larger expression.

preorder: A way to traverse a tree, visiting each node before its children.

prefix notation: A way of writing a mathematical expression with each operator appearing before its operands.

postorder: A way to traverse a tree, visiting the children of each node before the node itself.

inorder: A way to traverse a tree, visiting the left subtree, then the root, and then the right subtree.

Appendix A

Debugging

Different kinds of errors can occur in a program, and it is useful to distinguish among them in order to track them down more quickly:

- Syntax errors are produced by Python when it is translating the source code into byte code. They usually indicate that there is something wrong with the syntax of the program. Example: Omitting the colon at the end of a `def` statement yields the somewhat redundant message `SyntaxError: invalid syntax`.
- Runtime errors are produced by the runtime system if something goes wrong while the program is running. Most runtime error messages include information about where the error occurred and what functions were executing. Example: An infinite recursion eventually causes a runtime error of "maximum recursion depth exceeded."
- Semantic errors are problems with a program that compiles and runs but doesn't do the right thing. Example: An expression may not be evaluated in the order you expect, yielding an unexpected result.

The first step in debugging is to figure out which kind of error you are dealing with. Although the following sections are organized by error type, some techniques are applicable in more than one situation.

A.1 Syntax errors

Syntax errors are usually easy to fix once you figure out what they are. Unfortunately, the error messages are often not helpful. The most common messages are `SyntaxError: invalid syntax` and `SyntaxError: invalid token`, neither of which is very informative.

On the other hand, the message does tell you where in the program the problem occurred. Actually, it tells you where Python noticed a problem, which is not necessarily where the error is. Sometimes the error is prior to the location of the error message, often on the preceding line.

If you are building the program incrementally, you should have a good idea about where the error is. It will be in the last line you added.

If you are copying code from a book, start by comparing your code to the book's code very carefully. Check every character. At the same time, remember that the book might be wrong, so if you see something that looks like a syntax error, it might be.

Here are some ways to avoid the most common syntax errors:

1. Make sure you are not using a Python keyword for a variable name.

2. Check that you have a colon at the end of the header of every compound statement, including `for`, `while`, `if`, and `def` statements.

3. Check that indentation is consistent. You may indent with either spaces or tabs but it's best not to mix them. Each level should be nested the same amount.

4. Make sure that any strings in the code have matching quotation marks.

5. If you have multiline strings with triple quotes (single or double), make sure you have terminated the string properly. An unterminated string may cause an `invalid token` error at the end of your program, or it may treat the following part of the program as a string until it comes to the next string. In the second case, it might not produce an error message at all!

6. An unclosed bracket—`(`, `{`, or `[`—makes Python continue with the next line as part of the current statement. Generally, an error occurs almost immediately in the next line.

7. Check for the classic = instead of == inside a conditional.

If nothing works, move on to the next section...

A.1.1 I can't get my program to run no matter what I do.

If the compiler says there is an error and you don't see it, that might be because you and the compiler are not looking at the same code. Check your programming environment to make sure that the program you are editing is the one Python is trying to run. If you are not sure, try putting an obvious and deliberate syntax error at the beginning of the program. Now run (or import) it again. If the compiler doesn't find the new error, there is probably something wrong with the way your environment is set up.

If this happens, one approach is to start again with a new program like "Hello, World!," and make sure you can get a known program to run. Then gradually add the pieces of the new program to the working one.

A.2 Runtime errors

Once your program is syntactically correct, Python can import it and at least start running it. What could possibly go wrong?

A.2.1 My program does absolutely nothing.

This problem is most common when your file consists of functions and classes but does not actually invoke anything to start execution. This may be intentional if you only plan to import this module to supply classes and functions.

If it is not intentional, make sure that you are invoking a function to start execution, or execute one from the interactive prompt. Also see the "Flow of Execution" section below.

A.2.2 My program hangs.

If a program stops and seems to be doing nothing, we say it is "hanging." Often that means that it is caught in an infinite loop or an infinite recursion.

- If there is a particular loop that you suspect is the problem, add a `print` statement immediately before the loop that says "entering the loop" and another immediately after that says "exiting the loop."

  Run the program. If you get the first message and not the second, you've got an infinite loop. Go to the "Infinite Loop" section below.

- Most of the time, an infinite recursion will cause the program to run for a while and then produce a "RuntimeError: Maximum recursion depth exceeded" error. If that happens, go to the "Infinite Recursion" section below.

  If you are not getting this error but you suspect there is a problem with a recursive method or function, you can still use the techniques in the "Infinite Recursion" section.

- If neither of those steps works, start testing other loops and other recursive functions and methods.

- If that doesn't work, then it is possible that you don't understand the flow of execution in your program. Go to the "Flow of Execution" section below.

Infinite Loop

If you think you have an infinite loop and you think you know what loop is causing the problem, add a `print` statement at the end of the loop that prints the values of the variables in the condition and the value of the condition.

For example:

```
while x > 0 and y < 0 :
  # do something to x
  # do something to y

  print "x: ", x
  print  "y: ", y
  print  "condition: ", (x > 0 and y < 0)
```

Now when you run the program, you will see three lines of output for each time through the loop. The last time through the loop, the condition should be `false`. If the loop keeps going, you will be able to see the values of `x` and `y`, and you might figure out why they are not being updated correctly.

Infinite Recursion

Most of the time, an infinite recursion will cause the program to run for a while and then produce a `Maximum recursion depth exceeded` error.

If you suspect that a function or method is causing an infinite recursion, start by checking to make sure that there is a base case. In other words, there should be some condition that will cause the function or method to return without making a recursive invocation. If not, then you need to rethink the algorithm and identify a base case.

If there is a base case but the program doesn't seem to be reaching it, add a `print` statement at the beginning of the function or method that prints the parameters. Now when you run the program, you will see a few lines of output every time the function or method is invoked, and you will see the parameters. If the parameters are not moving toward the base case, you will get some ideas about why not.

Flow of Execution

If you are not sure how the flow of execution is moving through your program, add `print` statements to the beginning of each function with a message like "entering function `foo`," where `foo` is the name of the function.

Now when you run the program, it will print a trace of each function as it is invoked.

A.2.3 When I run the program I get an exception.

If something goes wrong during runtime, Python prints a message that includes the name of the exception, the line of the program where the problem occurred, and a traceback.

The traceback identifies the function that is currently running, and then the function that invoked it, and then the function that invoked *that*, and so on. In other words, it traces the path of function invocations that got you to where you are. It also includes the line number in your file where each of these calls occurs.

The first step is to examine the place in the program where the error occurred and see if you can figure out what happened. These are some of the most common runtime errors:

NameError: You are trying to use a variable that doesn't exist in the current environment. Remember that local variables are local. You cannot refer to them from outside the function where they are defined.

TypeError: There are several possible causes:

- You are trying to use a value improperly. Example: indexing a string, list, or tuple with something other than an integer.
- There is a mismatch between the items in a format string and the items passed for conversion. This can happen if either the number of items does not match or an invalid conversion is called for.

- You are passing the wrong number of arguments to a function or method. For methods, look at the method definition and check that the first parameter is `self`. Then look at the method invocation; make sure you are invoking the method on an object with the right type and providing the other arguments correctly.

KeyError: You are trying to access an element of a dictionary using a key value that the dictionary does not contain.

AttributeError: You are trying to access an attribute or method that does not exist.

IndexError: The index you are using to access a list, string, or tuple is greater than its length minus one. Immediately before the site of the error, add a `print` statement to display the value of the index and the length of the array. Is the array the right size? Is the index the right value?

A.2.4 I added so many `print` statements I get inundated with output.

One of the problems with using `print` statements for debugging is that you can end up buried in output. There are two ways to proceed: simplify the output or simplify the program.

To simplify the output, you can remove or comment out `print` statements that aren't helping, or combine them, or format the output so it is easier to understand.

To simplify the program, there are several things you can do. First, scale down the problem the program is working on. For example, if you are sorting an array, sort a *small* array. If the program takes input from the user, give it the simplest input that causes the problem.

Second, clean up the program. Remove dead code and reorganize the program to make it as easy to read as possible. For example, if you suspect that the problem is in a deeply nested part of the program, try rewriting that part with simpler structure. If you suspect a large function, try splitting it into smaller functions and testing them separately.

Often the process of finding the minimal test case leads you to the bug. If you find that a program works in one situation but not in another, that gives you a clue about what is going on.

Similarly, rewriting a piece of code can help you find subtle bugs. If you make a change that you think doesn't affect the program, and it does, that can tip you off.

A.3 Semantic errors

In some ways, semantic errors are the hardest to debug, because the compiler and the runtime system provide no information about what is wrong. Only you know what the program is supposed to do, and only you know that it isn't doing it.

The first step is to make a connection between the program text and the behavior you are seeing. You need a hypothesis about what the program is actually doing. One of the things that makes that hard is that computers run so fast.

You will often wish that you could slow the program down to human speed, and with some debuggers you can. But the time it takes to insert a few well-placed `print` statements is often short compared to setting up the debugger, inserting and removing breakpoints, and "walking" the program to where the error is occurring.

A.3.1 My program doesn't work.

You should ask yourself these questions:

- Is there something the program was supposed to do but which doesn't seem to be happening? Find the section of the code that performs that function and make sure it is executing when you think it should.

- Is something happening that shouldn't? Find code in your program that performs that function and see if it is executing when it shouldn't.

- Is a section of code producing an effect that is not what you expected? Make sure that you understand the code in question, especially if it involves invocations to functions or methods in other Python modules. Read the documentation for the functions you invoke. Try them out by writing simple test cases and checking the results.

In order to program, you need to have a mental model of how programs work. If you write a program that doesn't do what you expect, very often the problem is not in the program; it's in your mental model.

The best way to correct your mental model is to break the program into its components (usually the functions and methods) and test each component independently. Once you find the discrepancy between your model and reality, you can solve the problem.

Of course, you should be building and testing components as you develop the program. If you encounter a problem, there should be only a small amount of new code that is not known to be correct.

A.3.2 I've got a big hairy expression and it doesn't do what I expect.

Writing complex expressions is fine as long as they are readable, but they can be hard to debug. It is often a good idea to break a complex expression into a series of assignments to temporary variables.

For example:

```
self.hands[i].addCard (self.hands[self.findNeighbor(i)].popCard())
```

This can be rewritten as:

```
neighbor = self.findNeighbor (i)
pickedCard = self.hands[neighbor].popCard()
self.hands[i].addCard (pickedCard)
```

The explicit version is easier to read because the variable names provide additional documentation, and it is easier to debug because you can check the types of the intermediate variables and display their values.

Another problem that can occur with big expressions is that the order of evaluation may not be what you expect. For example, if you are translating the expression $\frac{x}{2\pi}$ into Python, you might write:

```
y = x / 2 * math.pi
```

That is not correct because multiplication and division have the same precedence and are evaluated from left to right. So this expression computes $x\pi/2$.

A good way to debug expressions is to add parentheses to make the order of evaluation explicit:

```
y = x / (2 * math.pi)
```

Whenever you are not sure of the order of evaluation, use parentheses. Not only will the program be correct (in the sense of doing what you intended), it will also be more readable for other people who haven't memorized the rules of precedence.

A.3.3 I've got a function or method that doesn't return what I expect.

If you have a `return` statement with a complex expression, you don't have a chance to print the `return` value before returning. Again, you can use a temporary variable. For example, instead of:

```
return self.hands[i].removeMatches()
```

you could write:

```
count = self.hands[i].removeMatches()
return count
```

Now you have the opportunity to display the value of `count` before returning.

A.3.4 I'm really, really stuck and I need help.

First, try getting away from the computer for a few minutes. Computers emit waves that affect the brain, causing these effects:

- Frustration and/or rage.
- Superstitious beliefs ("the computer hates me") and magical thinking ("the program only works when I wear my hat backward").
- Random-walk programming (the attempt to program by writing every possible program and choosing the one that does the right thing).

If you find yourself suffering from any of these symptoms, get up and go for a walk. When you are calm, think about the program. What is it doing? What are some possible causes of that behavior? When was the last time you had a working program, and what did you do next?

Sometimes it just takes time to find a bug. We often find bugs when we are away from the computer and let our minds wander. Some of the best places to find bugs are trains, showers, and in bed, just before you fall asleep.

A.3.5 No, I really need help.

It happens. Even the best programmers occasionally get stuck. Sometimes you work on a program so long that you can't see the error. A fresh pair of eyes is just the thing.

Before you bring someone else in, make sure you have exhausted the techniques described here. Your program should be as simple as possible, and you should be working on the smallest input that causes the error. You should have `print` statements in the appropriate places (and the output they produce should be comprehensible). You should understand the problem well enough to describe it concisely.

When you bring someone in to help, be sure to give them the information they need:

- If there is an error message, what is it and what part of the program does it indicate?
- What was the last thing you did before this error occurred? What were the last lines of code that you wrote, or what is the new test case that fails?
- What have you tried so far, and what have you learned?

When you find the bug, take a second to think about what you could have done to find it faster. Next time you see something similar, you will be able to find the bug more quickly.

Remember, the goal is not just to make the program work. The goal is to learn how to make the program work.

Appendix B

Creating a new data type

Object-oriented programming languages allow programmers to create new data types that behave much like built-in data types. We will explore this capability by building a `Fraction` class that works very much like the built-in numeric types: integers, longs and floats.

Fractions, also known as rational numbers, are values that can be expressed as a ratio of whole numbers, such as 5/6. The top number is called the numerator and the bottom number is called the denominator.

We start by defining a `Fraction` class with an initialization method that provides the numerator and denominator as integers:

```
class Fraction:
  def __init__(self, numerator, denominator=1):
    self.numerator = numerator
    self.denominator = denominator
```

The denominator is optional. A Fraction with just one parameter represents a whole number. If the numerator is n, we build the Fraction $n/1$.

The next step is to write a __str__ method that displays fractions in a way that makes sense. The form "numerator/denominator" is natural here:

```
class Fraction:
  ...
  def __str__(self):
    return "%d/%d" % (self.numerator, self.denominator)
```

To test what we have so far, we put it in a file named `Fraction.py` and import it into the Python interpreter. Then we create a fraction object and print it.

```
>>> from Fraction import Fraction
>>> spam = Fraction(5,6)
>>> print "The fraction is", spam
The fraction is 5/6
```

As usual, the `print` command invokes the __str__ method implicitly.

B.1 Fraction multiplication

We would like to be able to apply the normal addition, subtraction, multiplication, and division operations to fractions. To do this, we can overload the mathematical operators for `Fraction` objects.

We'll start with multiplication because it is the easiest to implement. To multiply fractions, we create a new fraction with a numerator that is the product of the original numerators and a denominator that is a product of the original denominators. __mul__ is the name Python uses for a method that overloads the * operator:

```
class Fraction:
  ...
  def __mul__(self, other):
    return Fraction(self.numerator*other.numerator,
                    self.denominator*other.denominator)
```

We can test this method by computing the product of two fractions:

```
>>> print Fraction(5,6) * Fraction(3,4)
15/24
```

It works, but we can do better! We can extend the method to handle multiplication by an integer. We use the `isinstance` function to test if `other` is an integer and convert it to a fraction if it is.

```
class Fraction:
  ...
  def __mul__(self, other):
    if isinstance(other, int):
      other = Fraction(other)
    return Fraction(self.numerator   * other.numerator,
                    self.denominator * other.denominator)
```

Multiplying fractions and integers now works, but only if the fraction is the left operand:

```
>>> print Fraction(5,6) * 4
20/6
>>> print 4 * Fraction(5,6)
TypeError: __mul__ nor __rmul__ defined for these operands
```

To evaluate a binary operator like multiplication, Python checks the left operand first to see if it provides a `__mul__` that supports the type of the second operand. In this case, the built-in integer operator doesn't support fractions.

Next, Python checks the right operand to see if it provides an `__rmul__` method that supports the first type. In this case, we haven't provided `__rmul__`, so it fails.

On the other hand, there is a simple way to provide `__rmul__`:

```
class Fraction:
  ...
  __rmul__ = __mul__
```

This assignment says that the `__rmul__` is the same as `__mul__`. Now if we evaluate `4 * Fraction(5,6)`, Python invokes `__rmul__` on the `Fraction` object and passes 4 as a parameter:

```
>>> print 4 * Fraction(5,6)
20/6
```

Since `__rmul__` is the same as `__mul__`, and `__mul__` can handle an integer parameter, we're all set.

B.2 Fraction addition

Addition is more complicated than multiplication, but still not too bad. The sum of a/b and c/d is the fraction `(a*d+c*b)/(b*d)`.

Using the multiplication code as a model, we can write `__add__` and `__radd__`:

```
class Fraction:
  ...
  def __add__(self, other):
    if isinstance(other, int):
      other = Fraction(other)
    return Fraction(self.numerator   * other.denominator +
                    self.denominator * other.numerator,
                    self.denominator * other.denominator)

  __radd__ = __add__
```

We can test these methods with `Fraction`s and integers.

```
>>> print Fraction(5,6) + Fraction(5,6)
60/36
>>> print Fraction(5,6) + 3
23/6
>>> print 2 + Fraction(5,6)
17/6
```

The first two examples invoke `__add__`; the last invokes `__radd__`.

B.3 Euclid's algorithm

In the previous example, we computed the sum $5/6 + 5/6$ and got 60/36. That is correct, but it's not the best way to represent the answer. To **reduce** the fraction to its simplest terms, we have to divide the numerator and denominator by their **greatest common divisor (GCD)**, which is 12. The result is 5/3.

In general, whenever we create a new `Fraction` object, we should reduce it by dividing the numerator and denominator by their GCD. If the fraction is already reduced, the GCD is 1.

Euclid of Alexandria (approx. 325–265 BCE) presented an algorithm to find the GCD for two integers m and n:

> If n divides m evenly, then n is the GCD. Otherwise the GCD is the GCD of n and the remainder of m divided by n.

This recursive definition can be expressed concisely as a function:

```
def gcd (m, n):
  if m % n == 0:
    return n
  else:
    return gcd(n, m%n)
```

In the first line of the body, we use the modulus operator to check divisibility. On the last line, we use it to compute the remainder after division.

Since all the operations we've written create new `Fraction`s for the result, we can reduce all results by modifying the initialization method.

```
class Fraction:
  def __init__(self, numerator, denominator=1):
    g = gcd (numerator, denominator)
    self.numerator   =    numerator / g
    self.denominator = denominator / g
```

Now whenever we create a `Fraction`, it is reduced to its simplest form:

```
>>> Fraction(100,-36)
-25/9
```

A nice feature of `gcd` is that if the fraction is negative, the minus sign is always moved to the numerator.

B.4 Comparing fractions

Suppose we have two `Fraction` objects, `a` and `b`, and we evaluate `a == b`. The default implementation of `==` tests for shallow equality, so it only returns true if `a` and `b` are the same object.

More likely, we want to return true if a and b have the same value—that is, deep equality.

We have to teach fractions how to compare themselves. As we saw in Section 15.4, we can overload all the comparison operators at once by supplying a `__cmp__` method.

By convention, the `__cmp__` method returns a negative number if `self` is less than `other`, zero if they are the same, and a positive number if `self` is greater than `other`.

The simplest way to compare fractions is to cross-multiply. If $a/b > c/d$, then $ad > bc$. With that in mind, here is the code for `__cmp__`:

```
class Fraction:
  ...
  def __cmp__(self, other):
    diff = (self.numerator  * other.denominator -
            other.numerator * self.denominator)
    return diff
```

If self is greater than other, then diff will be positive. If other is greater, then diff will be negative. If they are the same, diff is zero.

B.5 Taking it further

Of course, we are not done. We still have to implement subtraction by overriding __sub__ and division by overriding __div__.

One way to handle those operations is to implement negation by overriding __neg__ and inversion by overriding __invert__. Then we can subtract by negating the second operand and adding, and we can divide by inverting the second operand and multiplying.

Next, we have to provide __rsub__ and __rdiv__. Unfortunately, we can't use the same trick we used for addition and multiplication, because subtraction and division are not commutative. We can't just set __rsub__ and __rdiv__ equal to __sub__ and __div__. In these operations, the order of the operands makes a difference.

To handle **unary negation**, which is the use of the minus sign with a single operand, we override __neg__.

We can compute powers by overriding __pow__, but the implementation is a little tricky. If the exponent isn't an integer, then it may not be possible to represent the result as a Fraction. For example, Fraction(2) ** Fraction(1,2) is the square root of 2, which is an irrational number (it can't be represented as a fraction). So it's not easy to write the most general version of __pow__.

There is one other extension to the Fraction class that you might want to think about. So far, we have assumed that the numerator and denominator are integers.

> *As an exercise, finish the implementation of the* Fraction *class so that it handles subtraction, division and exponentiation.*

B.6 Glossary

greatest common divisor (GCD): The largest positive integer that divides without a remainder into both the numerator and denominator of a fraction.

reduce: To change a fraction into an equivalent form with a GCD of 1.

unary negation: The operation that computes an additive inverse, usually denoted with a leading minus sign. Called "unary" by contrast with the binary minus operation, which is subtraction.

reduce: To change a fraction into an equivalent form with a GCD of 1.

unary negation: The operation that computes an additive inverse, usually denoted with a leading minus sign. Called "unary" by contrast with the binary minus operation, which is subtraction.

Appendix C

Recommendations for further reading

So where do you go from here? There are many directions to pursue, extending your knowledge of Python specifically and computer science in general.

The examples in this book have been deliberately simple, but they may not have shown off Python's most exciting capabilities. Here is a sampling of extensions to Python and suggestions for projects that use them.

- GUI (graphical user interface) programming lets your program use a windowing environment to interact with the user and display graphics.

  The oldest graphics package for Python is Tkinter, which is based on Jon Ousterhout's Tcl and Tk scripting languages. Tkinter comes bundled with the Python distribution.

  Another popular platform is wxPython, which is essentially a Python veneer over wxWindows, a C++ package which in turn implements windows using native interfaces on Windows and Unix (including Linux) platforms. The windows and controls under wxPython tend to have a more native look and feel than those of Tkinter and are somewhat simpler to program.

  Any type of GUI programming will lead you into event-driven programming, where the user and not the programmer determines the flow of execution. This style of programming takes some getting used to, sometimes forcing you to rethink the whole structure of a program.

- Web programming integrates Python with the Internet. For example, you can build web client programs that open and read a remote web page (almost) as easily as you can open a file on disk. There are also Python modules that let you access remote files via ftp, and modules to let you send and receive email. Python is also widely used for web server programs to handle input forms.

- Databases are a bit like super files where data is stored in predefined schemas, and relationships between data items let you access the data in various ways. Python has several modules to enable users to connect to various database engines, both Open Source and commercial.

- Thread programming lets you run several threads of execution within a single program. If you have had the experience of using a web browser to scroll the beginning of a page while the browser continues to load the rest of it, then you have a feel for what threads can do.

- When speed is paramount Python extensions may be written in a compiled language like C or C++. Such extensions form the base of many of the modules in the Python library. The mechanics of linking functions and data is somewhat complex. SWIG (Simplified Wrapper and Interface Generator) is a tool to make the process much simpler.

C.1 Python-related web sites and books

Here are the authors' recommendations for Python resources on the web:

- The Python home page at `www.python.org` is the place to start your search for any Python related material. You will find help, documentation, links to other sites and SIG (Special Interest Group) mailing lists that you can join.

- The Open Book Project `www.ibiblio.com/obp` contains not only this book online but also similar books for Java and C++ by Allen Downey. In addition there are *Lessons in Electric Circuits* by Tony R. Kuphaldt, *Getting down with ...*, a set of tutorials on a range of computer science topics, written and edited by high school students, *Python for Fun*, a set of case studies in Python by Chris Meyers, and *The Linux Cookbook* by Michael Stultz, with 300 pages of tips and techniques.

- Finally if you go to Google and use the search string "python -snake -monty" you will get about 750,000 hits.

And here are some books that contain more material on the Python language:

- *Core Python Programming* by Wesley Chun is a large book at about 750 pages. The first part of the book covers the basic Python language features. The second part provides an easy-paced introduction to more advanced topics including many of those mentioned above.

- *Python Essential Reference* by David M. Beazley is a small book, but it is packed with information both on the language itself and the modules in the standard library. It is also very well indexed.

- *Python Pocket Reference* by Mark Lutz really does fit in your pocket. Although not as extensive as *Python Essential Reference* it is a handy reference for the most commonly used functions and modules. Mark Lutz is also the author of *Programming Python*, one of the earliest (and largest) books on Python and not aimed at the beginning programmer. His later book *Learning Python* is smaller and more accessible.

- *Python Programming on Win32* by Mark Hammond and Andy Robinson is a "must have" for anyone seriously using Python to develop Windows applications. Among other things it covers the integration of Python and COM, builds a small application with wxPython, and even uses Python to script windows applications such as Word and Excel.

C.2 Recommended general computer science books

The following suggestions for further reading include many of the authors' favorite books. They deal with good programming practices and computer science in general.

- *The Practice of Programming* by Kernighan and Pike covers not only the design and coding of algorithms and data structures, but also debugging, testing and improving the performance of programs. The examples are mostly C++ and Java, with none in Python.

- *The Elements of Java Style* edited by Al Vermeulen is another small book that discusses some of the finer points of good programming, such as good use of naming conventions, comments, and even whitespace and indentation (somewhat of a nonissue in Python). The book also covers programming by contract, using assertions to catch errors by testing preconditions and postconditions, and proper programming with threads and their synchronization.

- *Programming Pearls* by Jon Bentley is a classic book. It consists of case studies that originally appeared in the author's column in the *Communications of the ACM.* The studies deal with tradeoffs in programming and why it is often an especially bad idea to run with your first idea for a program. The book is a bit older than those above (1986), so the examples are in older languages. There are lots of problems to solve, some with solutions and others with hints. This book was very popular and was followed by a second volume.

- *The New Turing Omnibus* by A.K Dewdney provides a gentle introduction to 66 topics of computer science ranging from parallel computing to computer viruses, from cat scans to genetic algorithms. All of the topics are short and entertaining. An earlier book by Dewdney *The Armchair Universe* is a collection from his column *Computer Recreations* in *Scientific American.* Both books are a rich source of ideas for projects.

- *Turtles, Termites and Traffic Jams* by Mitchel Resnick is about the power of decentralization and how complex behavior can arise from coordinated simple activity of a multitude of agents. It introduces the language StarLogo, which allows the user to write programs for the agents. Running the program demonstrates complex aggregate behavior, which is often counterintuitive. Many of the programs in the book were developed by students in middle school and high school. Similar programs could be written in Python using simple graphics and threads.

- *Gödel, Escher and Bach* by Douglas Hofstadter. Put simply, if you found magic in recursion you will also find it in this bestselling book. One of Hofstadter's themes involves "strange loops" where patterns evolve and ascend until they meet themselves again. It is Hofstadter's contention that such "strange loops" are an essential part of what separates the animate from the inanimate. He demonstrates such patterns in the music of Bach, the pictures of Escher and Gödel's incompleteness theorem.

Index

Make Way for Ducklings, 75
Python Library Reference, 81

abecedarian, 75
abstract class, 206
abstract data type, *see* ADT
access, 84
accumulator, 164, 167, 176
addition
    fraction, 234
ADT, 191, 196, 197
    Priority Queue, 199, 203
    Queue, 199
    Stack, 192
algorithm, 9, 144, 145
aliasing, 92, 96, 110, 135
ambiguity, 7, 131
    fundamental theorem, 186
animal game, 216
append method, 163
argument, 23, 30, 35
arithmetic sequence, 65
assignment, 12, 21, 61
    multiple , 72
    tuple, 98, 105, 166
attribute, 130, 137
    class, 161, 167
AttributeError, 226

base case, 44, 47
binary operator, 209, 219
binary tree, 207, 219
block, 39, 47
body, 39, 47
    loop, 63
boolean expression, 37, 47
boolean function, 54, 167
bracket operator, 73
branch, 40, 47
break statement, 119, 126
bug, 4, 9

call
    function, 23
call graph, 112
Card, 159
cargo, 181, 190, 207
chained conditional, 40
character, 73
character classification, 80
child class, 169, 179
child node, 207, 219
circular buffer, 206
circular definition, 55
class, 129, 137
    Card, 159
    Golfer, 205
    LinkedList, 188
    Node, 181
    OldMaidGame, 175
    OldMaidHand, 173
    parent, 170, 172
    Point, 153
    Stack, 192
class attribute, 161, 167
classification
    character, 80
client, 192, 197

clone, 96
cloning, 92, 110
coercion, 35
  type, 24, 113
collection, 183, 192
column, 95
comment, 19, 21
comparable, 162
comparison
  fraction, 235
  string, 76
compile, 2, 9
compile-time error, 221
compiler, 221
complete language, 55
complete ordering, 162
composition, 19, 21, 26, 53, 159, 163
compound data type, 73, 81, 129
compound statement, 39, 47
  body, 39
  header, 39
  statement block, 39
compression, 113
computational pattern, 78
concatenation, 18, 21, 75, 77
  list, 87
condition, 47, 63, 224
conditional
  chained, 40
conditional branching, 39
conditional execution, 39
conditional operator, 162
conditional statement, 47
constant time, 201, 206
constructor, 129, 137, 160
continue statement, 120, 126
conversion
  type, 24
copy module, 135
copying, 110, 135
counter, 78, 81
counting, 101, 113
cursor, 72

data structure
  generic, 192, 193
  recursive, 181, 190, 208
data type
  compound, 73, 129
  dictionary, 107
  immutable, 97
  long integer, 113
  tuple, 97
  user-defined, 129, 231
dead code, 50, 60
dealing cards, 171
debugging, 4, 9, 221
deck, 163
decrement, 81
deep copy, 137
deep equality, 132, 137
definition
  circular, 55
  function, 27
  recursive, 214
deletion
  list, 89
delimiter, 96, 123, 194, 197
denominator, 231
deterministic, 105
development
  incremental, 51, 145
  planned, 145
development plan, 72
dictionary, 95, 107, 115, 122, 226
  method, 109
  operation, 108
directory, 123, 126
division
  integer, 24
documentation, 190
dot notation, 25, 35, 109, 149, 152
dot product, 154, 158
Doyle, Arthur Conan, 5

element, 83, 96
embedded reference, 136, 181, 190, 207
encapsulate, 72
encapsulation, 67, 134, 191, 196
encode, 160, 167
encrypt, 160
equality, 132
error
  compile-time, 221
  runtime, 5, 45, 221
  semantic, 5, 221, 227
  syntax, 4, 221
error checking, 58
error handling, 216
error messages, 221
escape sequence, 66, 72
Euclid, 234
eureka traversal, 78
except statement, 124, 126
exception, 5, 9, 124, 126, 221, 225
executable, 9
execution
  flow, 225
expression, 17, 21, 194
  big and hairy, 228
  boolean, 37, 47
expression tree, 209, 212

factorial function, 55, 58
Fibonacci function, 58, 111
FIFO, 199, 206
file, 117, 126
  text, 119
float, 11
floating-point, 21, 129
flow of execution, 29, 35, 225
for loop, 74, 86
formal language, 6, 9
format operator, 120, 126, 205, 225
format string, 120, 126
frabjuous, 55
fraction, 231
  addition, 234
  comparison, 235
  multiplication, 232
frame, 32, 35, 44, 112
function, 27, 35, 71, 139, 148
  argument, 30
  boolean, 54, 167
  composition, 26, 53
  factorial, 55
  helper, 187
  math, 25
  parameter, 30
  recursive, 44
  tuple as return value, 99
  wrapper, 187
function call, 23, 35
function definition, 27, 35
function frame, 32, 35, 44, 112
function type
  modifier, 141
  pure, 140
functional programming style, 142, 145
fundamental ambiguity theorem, 190

game
  animal, 216
gamma function, 59
generalization, 67, 134, 144
generalize, 72
generic data structure, 192, 193
geometric sequence, 65
Golfer, 205
greatest common divisor, 234, 237
guardian, 60

handle exception, 124, 126
handling errors, 216
hanging, 223
hello world, 8
helper function, 187
helper method, 190
high-level language, 2, 9
hint, 111, 115
histogram, 104, 105, 113

Holmes, Sherlock, 5

identity, 132
immutable, 97
immutable string, 77
immutable type, 105
implementation
  Queue, 199
improved queue, 201
in operator, 86, 166
increment, 81
incremental development, 51, 60, 145
incremental program development, 222
index, 74, 81, 96, 107, 225
  negative, 74
IndexError, 226
infinite list, 185
infinite loop, 63, 72, 223, 224
infinite recursion, 45, 47, 59, 223, 224
infix, 194, 197, 209
inheritance, 169, 179
initialization method, 152, 158, 163
inorder, 210, 219
instance, 131, 134, 137
  object, 130, 148, 162
instantiate, 137
instantiation, 130
int, 11
integer
  long, 113
integer division, 17, 20, 21, 24
Intel, 64
interface, 192, 206
interpret, 2, 9
invariant, 189, 190
invoke, 115
invoking method, 109
irrational, 236
iteration, 61, 62, 72

join function, 95

key, 107, 115
key-value pair, 107, 115
KeyError, 226
keyword, 13, 15, 21
knowledge base, 216

language, 131
  complete, 55
  formal, 6
  high-level, 2
  low-level, 2
  natural, 6
  programming, 1
  safe, 5
leaf node, 207, 219
leap of faith, 57, 184
length, 85
level, 207, 219
linear time, 201, 206
link, 190
linked list, 181, 190
linked queue, 200, 206
LinkedList, 188
Linux, 6
list, 83, 96, 181
  as argument, 183
  as parameter, 93
  cloning, 92
  element, 84
  for loop, 86
  infinite, 185
  length, 85
  linked, 181, 190
  loop, 185
  membership, 86
  modifying, 186
  mutable, 88
  nested, 83, 94, 110
  of objects, 163
  printing, 183
  printing backwards, 184
  slice, 88
  traversal, 85, 183
  traverse recursively, 184

well-formed, 189
list deletion, 89
list method, 114, 163
list operation, 87
list traversal, 96
literalness, 7
local variable, 31, 35, 69
logarithm, 64
logical operator, 37, 38
long integer, 113
loop, 63, 72
body, 63, 72
condition, 224
for loop, 74
in list, 185
infinite, 63, 224
nested, 163
traversal, 74
while, 62
loop variable, 72, 171, 183
low-level language, 2, 9
lowercase, 80

map to, 160
math function, 25
mathematical operator, 232
matrix, 94
sparse, 110
McCloskey, Robert, 75
mental model, 227
method, 109, 115, 139, 148, 158
dictionary, 109
initialization, 152, 163
invocation, 109
list, 114, 163
model
mental, 227
modifier, 141, 145
modifying lists, 186
module, 25, 35, 79
copy, 135
string, 80
modulus operator, 37, 47, 171
multiple assignment, 61, 72
multiplication
fraction, 232
mutable, 77, 81, 97
list, 88
object, 134
mutable type, 105

NameError, 225
natural language, 6, 9, 131
negation, 236
nested list, 94, 96, 110
nested structure, 159
nesting, 47
newline, 72
node, 181, 190, 207, 219
Node class, 181
None, 50, 60
number
random, 99
numerator, 231

object, 91, 96, 129, 137
list of, 163
mutable, 134
object code, 9
object instance, 130, 148, 162
object invariant, 189
object-oriented design, 169
object-oriented programming, 147, 169
object-oriented programming language, 147, 158
operand, 17, 21
operation
dictionary, 108
list, 87
operator, 17, 21
binary, 209, 219
bracket, 73
conditional, 162
format, 120, 126, 205, 225
in, 86, 166
logical, 37, 38

modulus, 37, 171
overloading, 154, 232
operator overloading, 154, 158, 162, 205
order of evaluation, 228
order of operations, 17
ordering, 162
overload, 232
overloading, 158
operator, 205
override, 158, 162

parameter, 30, 35, 93, 131
list, 93
parent class, 169, 170, 172, 179
parent node, 207, 219
parse, 7, 9, 194, 197, 212
partial ordering, 162
pass statement, 39
path, 123
pattern, 78
pattern matching, 105
Pentium, 64
performance, 201
performance hazard, 206
pickle, 126
pickling, 123
planned development, 145
poetry, 7
Point class, 153
polymorphic, 158
polymorphism, 155
pop, 193
portability, 9
portable, 2
postfix, 194, 197, 209
postorder, 210, 219
precedence, 21, 228
precondition, 185, 190
prefix, 210, 219
preorder, 210, 219
print statement, 8, 9, 226
printing
deck object, 163
hand of cards, 171
object, 131, 148
priority, 205
priority queue, 199, 206
ADT, 203
priority queueing, 199
problem-solving, 9
product, 214
program, 9
development, 72
program development
encapsulation, 67
generalization, 67
programming language, 1
prompt, 45, 47
prose, 7
prototype development, 143
provider, 192, 197
pseudocode, 234
pseudorandom, 105
pure function, 140, 145
push, 193

queue, 199, 206
improved implementation, 201
linked implementation, 200
List implementation, 199
Queue ADT, 199
queueing policy, 199, 206

raise exception, 124, 126
random, 165
random number, 99
randrange, 165
rank, 159
rational, 231
rectangle, 133
recursion, 42, 44, 47, 55, 57, 209, 210
base case, 44
infinite, 45, 59, 224
recursive data structure, 181, 190, 208
recursive definition, 214
reduce, 234, 237

redundancy, 7
reference, 181
  aliasing, 92
  embedded, 136, 181, 190
regular expression, 194
removing cards, 166
repetition
  list, 87
return statement, 42, 228
return value, 23, 35, 49, 60, 134
  tuple, 99
role
  variable, 186
root node, 207, 219
row, 95
rules of precedence, 17, 21
runtime error, 5, 9, 45, 74, 77, 85, 98, 109, 111, 118, 121, 221, 225

safe language, 5
sameness, 131
scaffolding, 50, 60
scalar multiplication, 154, 158
script, 9
semantic error, 5, 9, 99, 221, 227
semantics, 5, 9
sequence, 83, 96
shallow copy, 137
shallow equality, 132, 137
shuffle, 165
sibling node, 219
singleton, 187, 188, 190
slice, 76, 81, 88
source code, 9
split function, 95
Stack, 192
stack, 192
stack diagram, 32, 35, 44
state diagram, 12, 21
statement, 21
  assignment, 12, 61
  block, 39
  break, 119, 126
  compound, 39
  conditional, 47
  continue, 120, 126
  except, 124
  pass, 39
  print, 8, 9, 226
  return, 42, 228
  try, 124
  while, 62
straight flush, 172
string, 11
  immutable, 77
  length, 74
  slice, 76
string comparison, 76
string module, 79, 80
string operation, 18
subclass, 169, 172, 179
subexpression, 215
suit, 159
sum, 214
swap, 166
syntax, 4, 9, 222
syntax error, 4, 9, 221

tab, 72
table, 64
  two-dimensional, 66
temporary variable, 50, 60, 228
text file, 119, 126
theorem
  fundamental ambiguity, 186
token, 9, 194, 197, 212
traceback, 33, 35, 45, 125, 225
traversal, 74, 78, 86, 174
  list, 85
traverse, 81, 183, 184, 204, 209, 210
tree, 207
  empty, 208
  expression, 209, 212
  traversal, 209, 210
tree node, 207
try, 126

try statement, 124
tuple, 97, 99, 105
tuple assignment, 98, 105, 166
Turing Thesis, 55
Turing, Alan, 55
type, 11, 21
  dict, 107
  file, 117
  float, 11
  int, 11
  list, 83
  long, 113
  str, 11
  tuple, 97
type checking, 58
type coercion, 24, 113
type conversion, 24
TypeError, 225

unary negation, 237
unary operator, 236
underscore character, 13
uppercase, 80
user-defined data type, 129

value, 11, 21, 91
  tuple, 99
variable, 12, 21
  local, 31, 69
  loop, 171
  roles, 186
  temporary, 50, 60, 228
veneer, 193, 206

while statement, 62
whitespace, 80, 81
wrapper, 190
wrapper function, 187